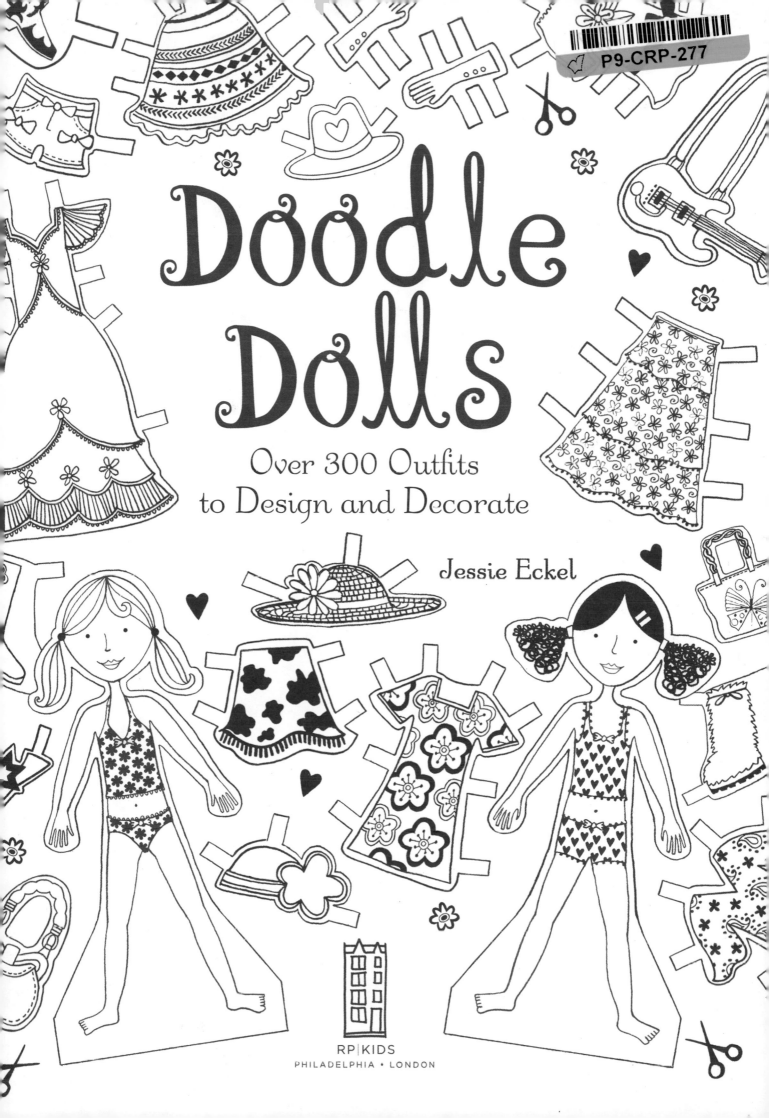

Doodle Dolls

Over 300 Outfits to Design and Decorate

Jessie Eckel

RP | KIDS

PHILADELPHIA • LONDON

First published in Great Britain by Buster Books,
an imprint of Michael O'Mara Books Limited, 2009

First published in the United States
by Running Press Book Publishers, 2010

Printed in China

9 8 7 6 5 4
Digit on the right indicates the number of this printing

ISBN 978-0-7624-3819-8

Illustrated by Jessie Eckel

This edition published by Running Press Kids,
an imprint of Running Press Book Publishers
2300 Chestnut Street
Philadelphia, PA 19103-4371

Visit us on the web!
www.runningpress.com

All About This Book

Inside the front and back cover of this book you will find Miah and Cherry. They are your doodle dolls. They love to try on different outfits and can't wait for your creations!

Miah

Cherry

How To Begin

DOLL STAND   DOLL BASE

Glue here

First you need to help the dolls stand up.

1. Turn to the inside-front cover and punch out the white strip—this is the doll stand.

2. Punch out Miah's solid outline carefully. You could ask an adult for help with this bit, as it can be quite tricky.

3. Fold the strip back along each dotted line.

4. Use a glue stick to dab a little glue on to the ends of the strip.

5. Stick the ends of the strip to the doll base, where marked, and leave to dry.

6. Turn to the inside-back cover and repeat steps one to five for Cherry.

Glue here   Stick here

Doodle Doll Outfits

The book is filled with clothes for your dolls to wear and share—from fancy-dress costumes and party wear, to skating outfits and swimsuits. Each item of clothing has two sides. One side has a pretty pattern for you to color in, and the other side is blank for you to doodle and decorate a design yourself.

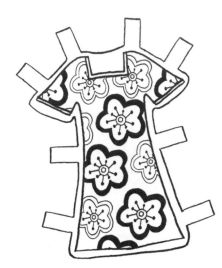
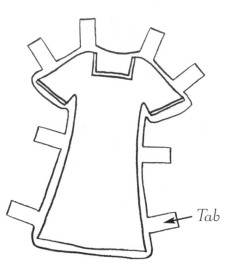

Tab

Dressing Your Dolls

1. Cut around the solid outline of each item of clothing. Make sure that you cut around the tabs carefully.

2. Decorate the outfits in colors of your choice, or doodle pretty patterns to really make your dolls stand out. You could even add glitter for some extra glamour.

3. To dress your dolls, simply fold the tabs around their bodies. Layer the outfits in different combinations to create a unique look.

TOP TIP. Take extra care when cutting out the bags. Cut around the solid outline as usual, then ask an adult to cut out the center of the handle for you.

You will then be able to slip the doodle dolls' hands through the handles.

Cut out here.

The Doodle Dolls' Wardrobe

In the middle of this book, you will find the front and back of your dolls' wardrobe. You can use this wardrobe envelope to store the dolls' clothes in.

1. Gently punch out the front and the back pieces.

2. Fold along the grey dotted lines of tab A, B, and C on the back piece.

3. Using a glue stick, dab glue along each tab.

4. Lay the front piece on top of the tabs, so the lock and slot line up. Leave your wardrobe envelope to dry completely.

5. Once your wardrobe envelope has dried, color and decorate it.

6. On the front piece, fold the flap over along the grey dotted line and tuck the lock into the slot to close.

When it is complete, pop the dolls' clothes inside to keep them safe.

DOODLE DOLLS OUT AND ABOUT!

They like summer style for sunny days.

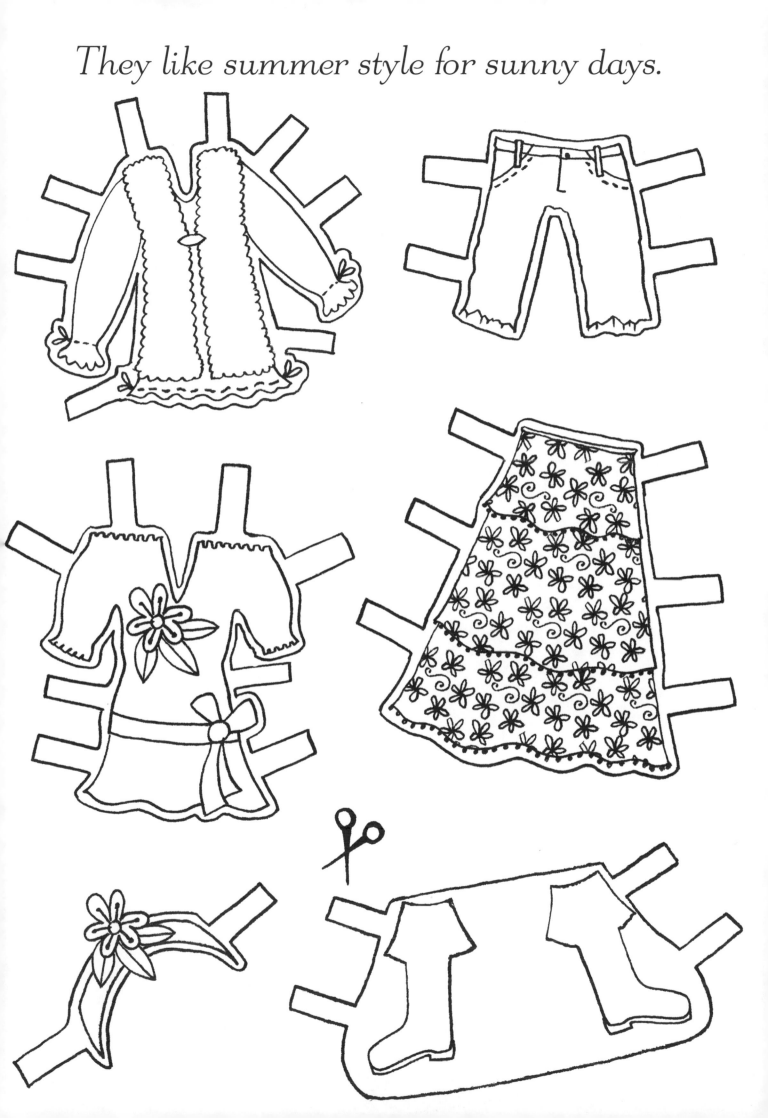

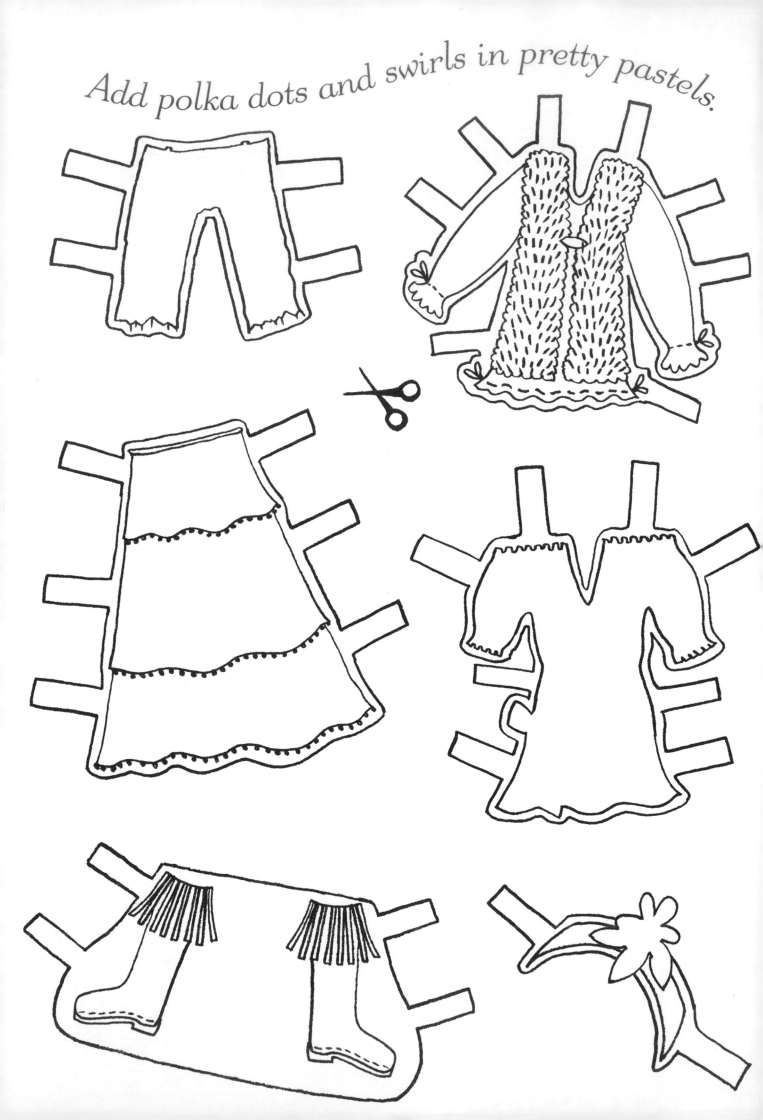

Add polka dots and swirls in pretty pastels.

Pretty flowers and paisley are super-cool.

Add bold and bright patterns.

The "Queen of Shopping" steps out.

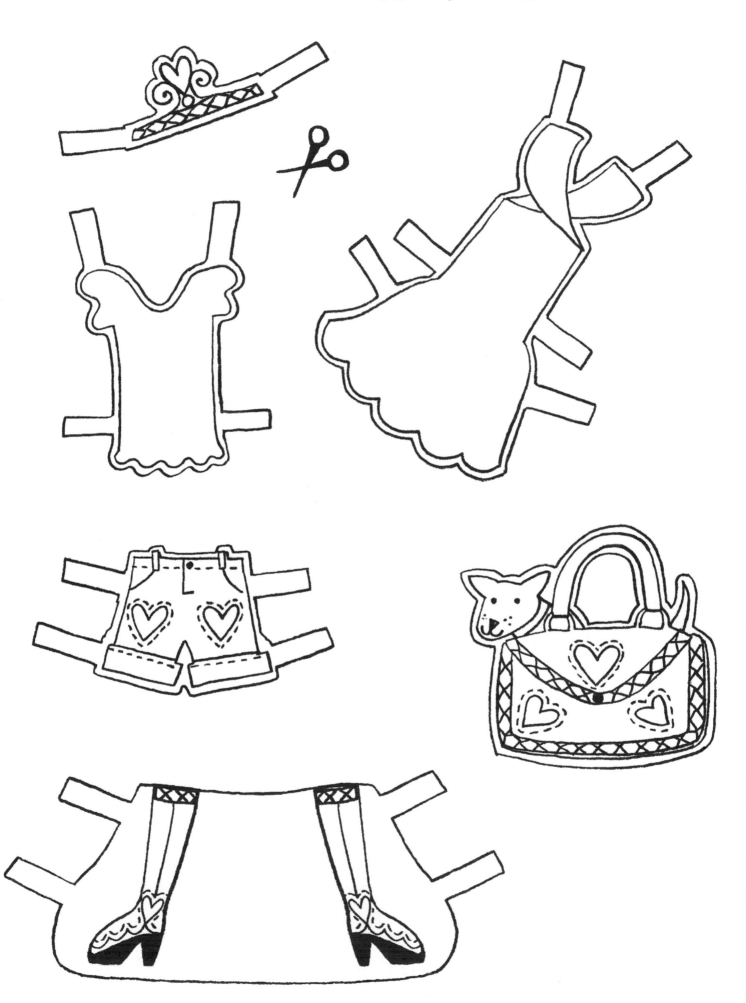

Add huge hearts and fun flowers.

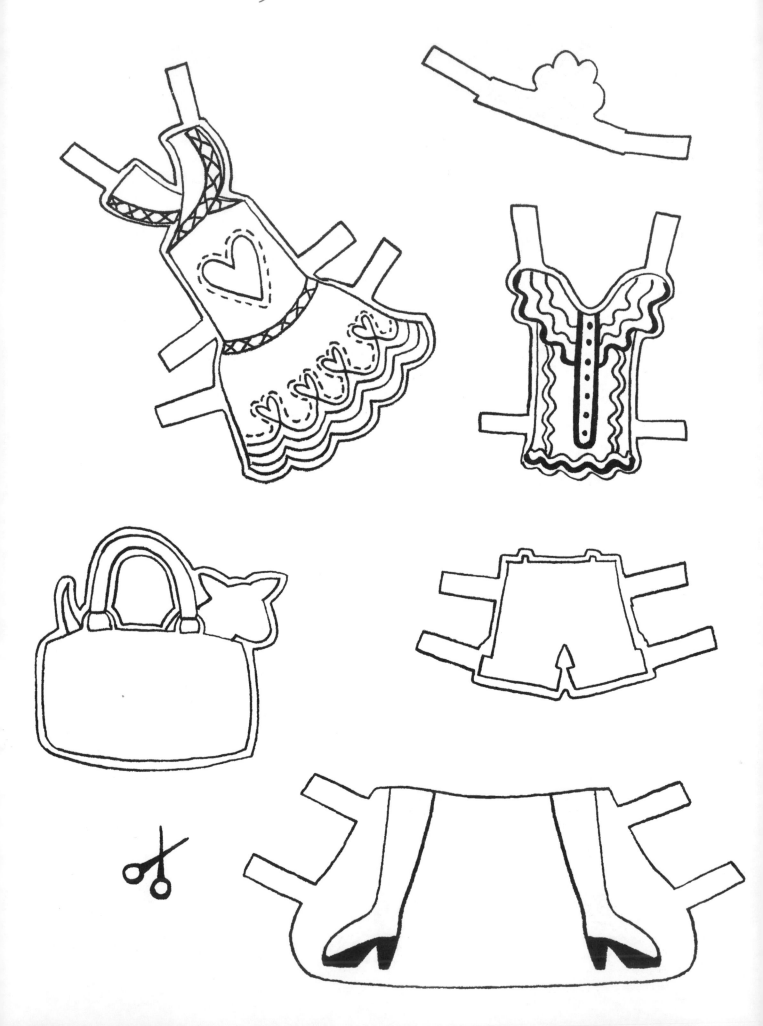

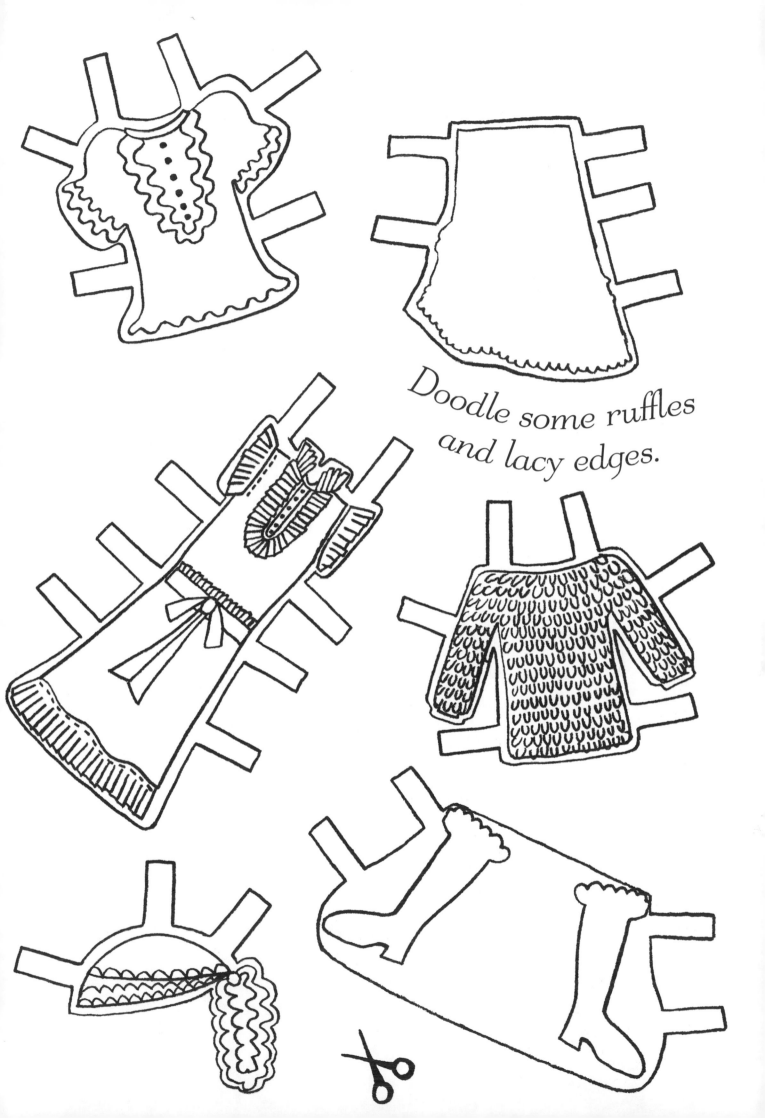

Doodle some ruffles and lacy edges.

Why not add some pretty frills and ribbons?

Get Miah ready for school.

Add smart stripes and checks.

Cherry loves playing football.

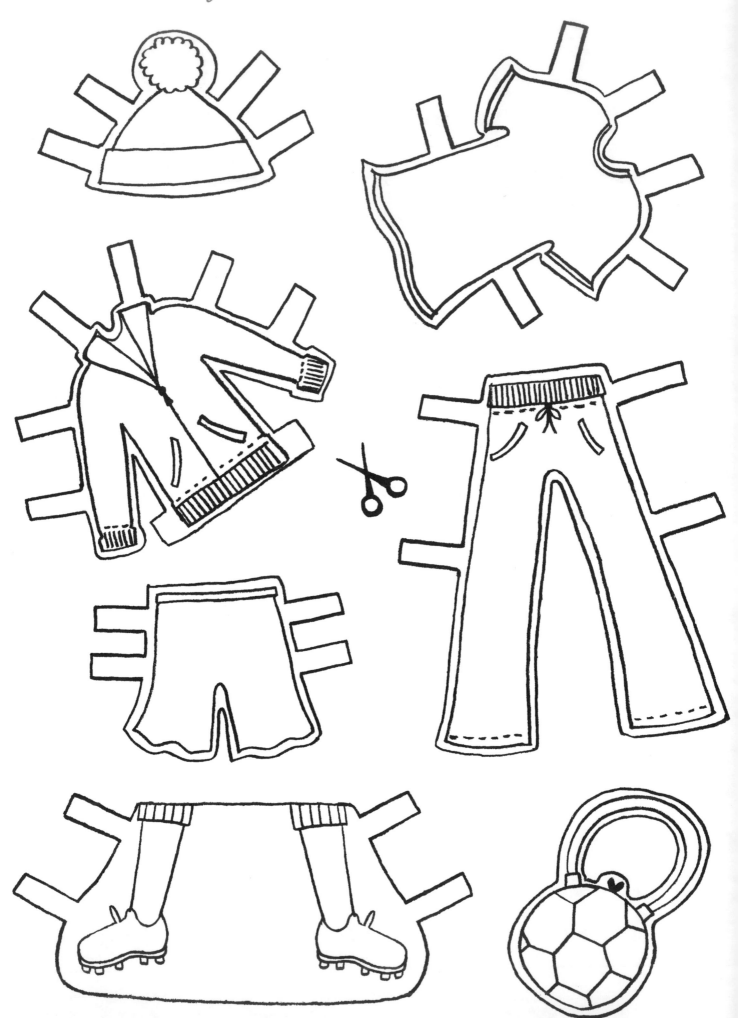

Wrap the dolls up in cozy clothes.

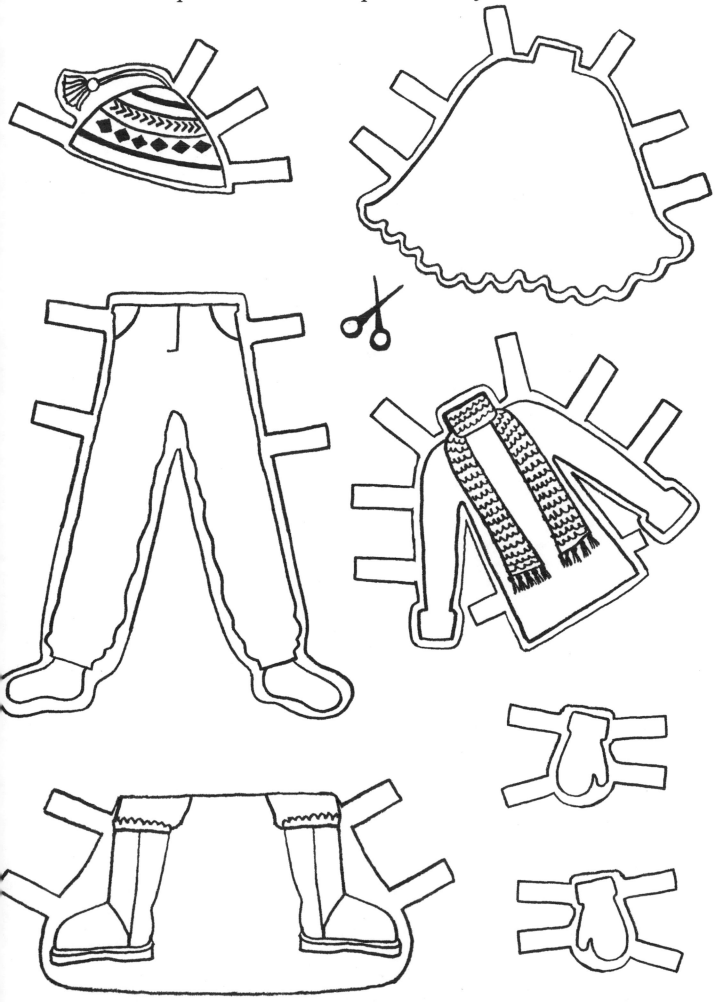

Brighten winter days with colorful clothes.

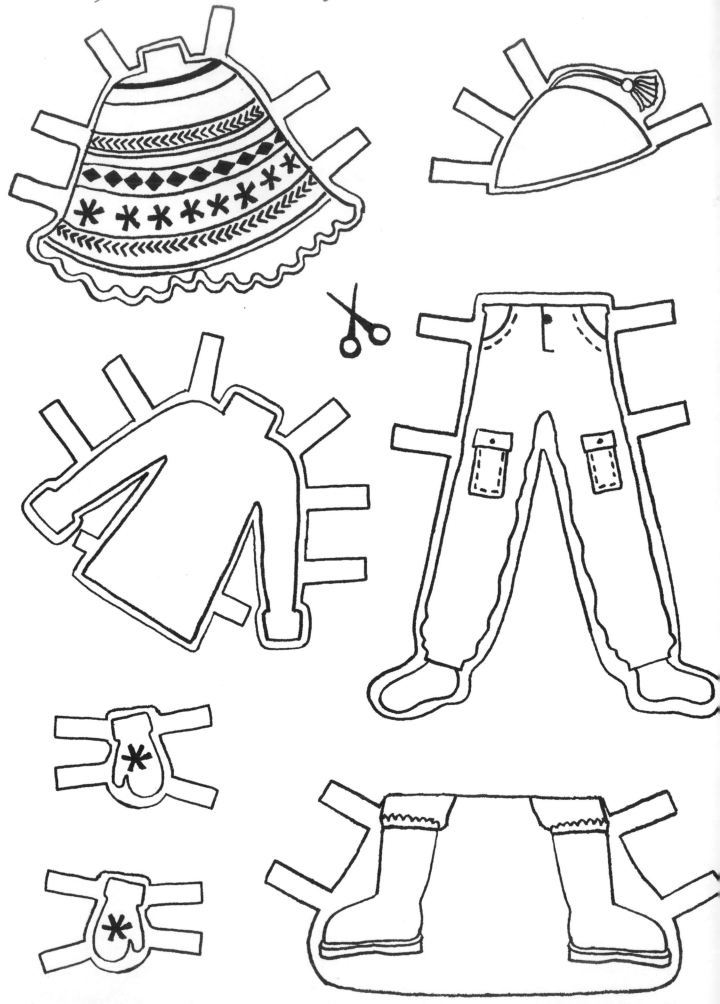

The dolls love to play at the beach.

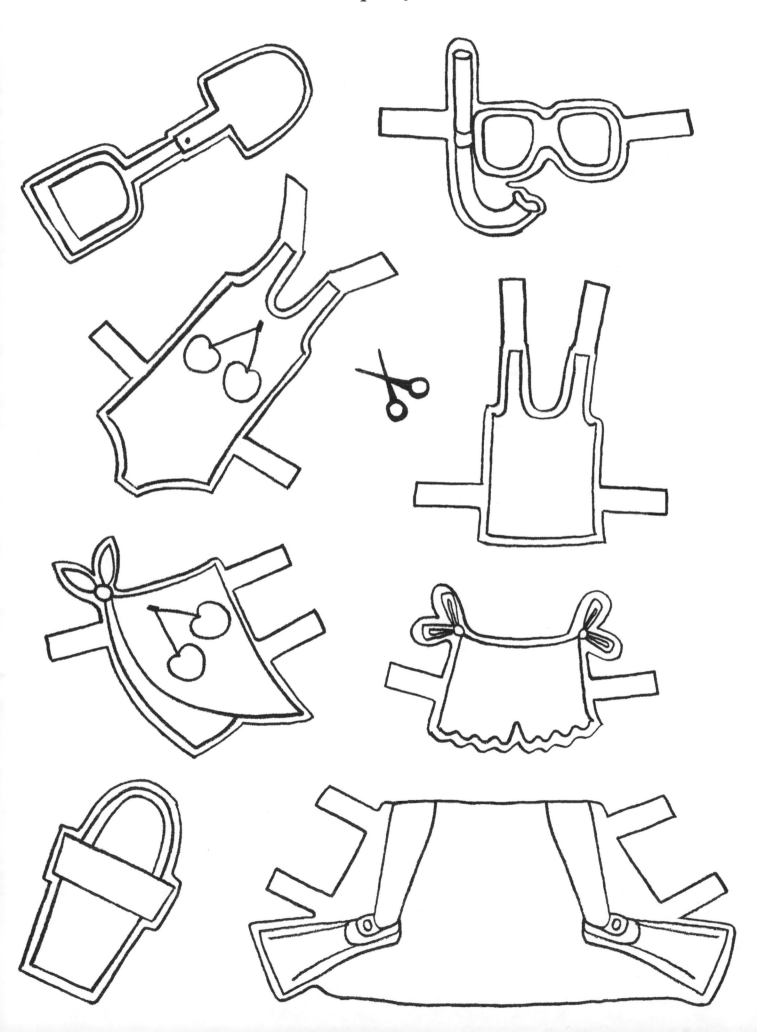

Complete the beachwear with sunny colors.

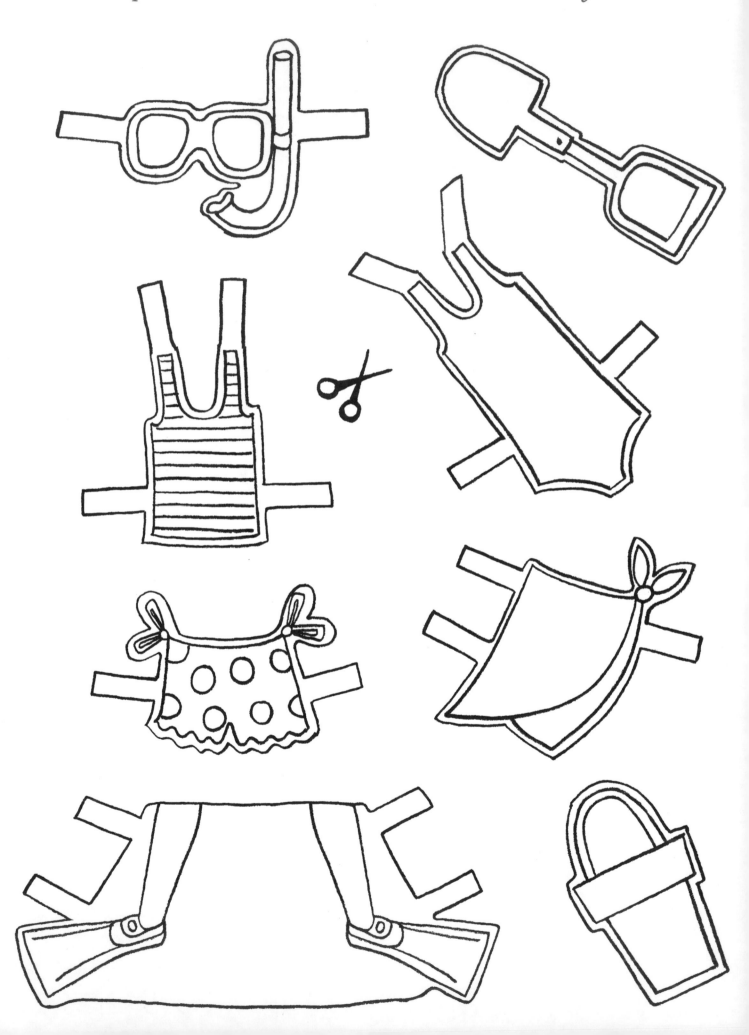

Doodle the dolls great clothes for the sunshine.

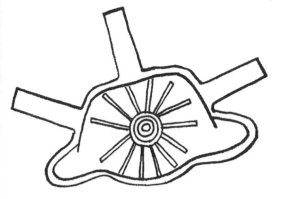
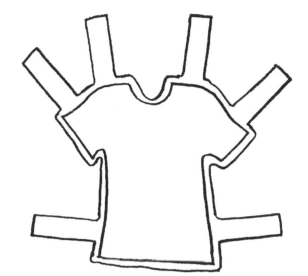
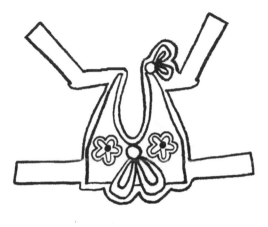

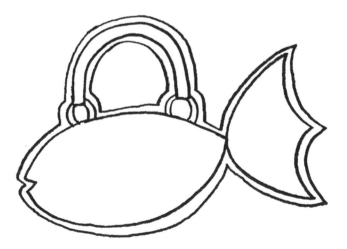
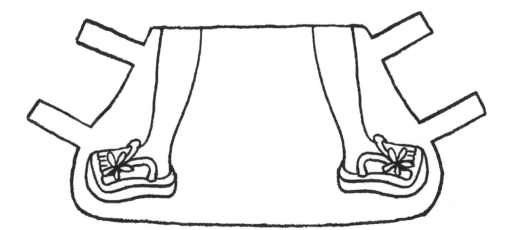

Perfect for the sea and sand.

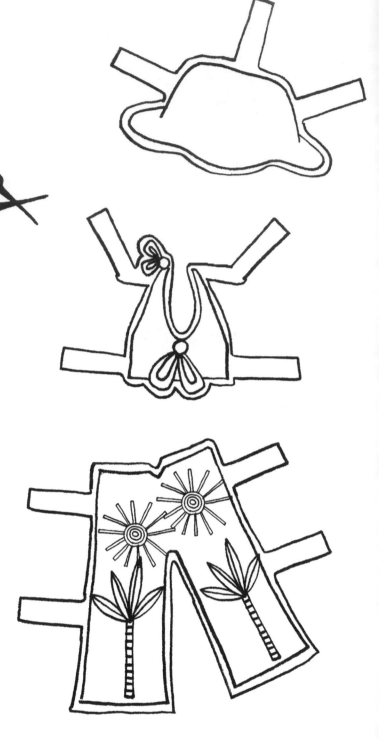
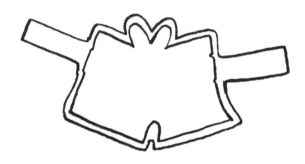
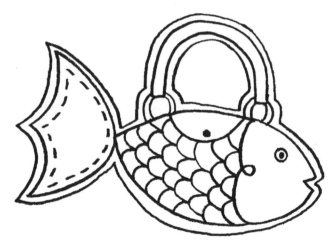
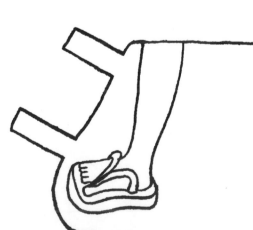
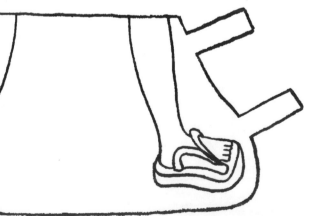

Make Miah a seaworthy sailor suit.

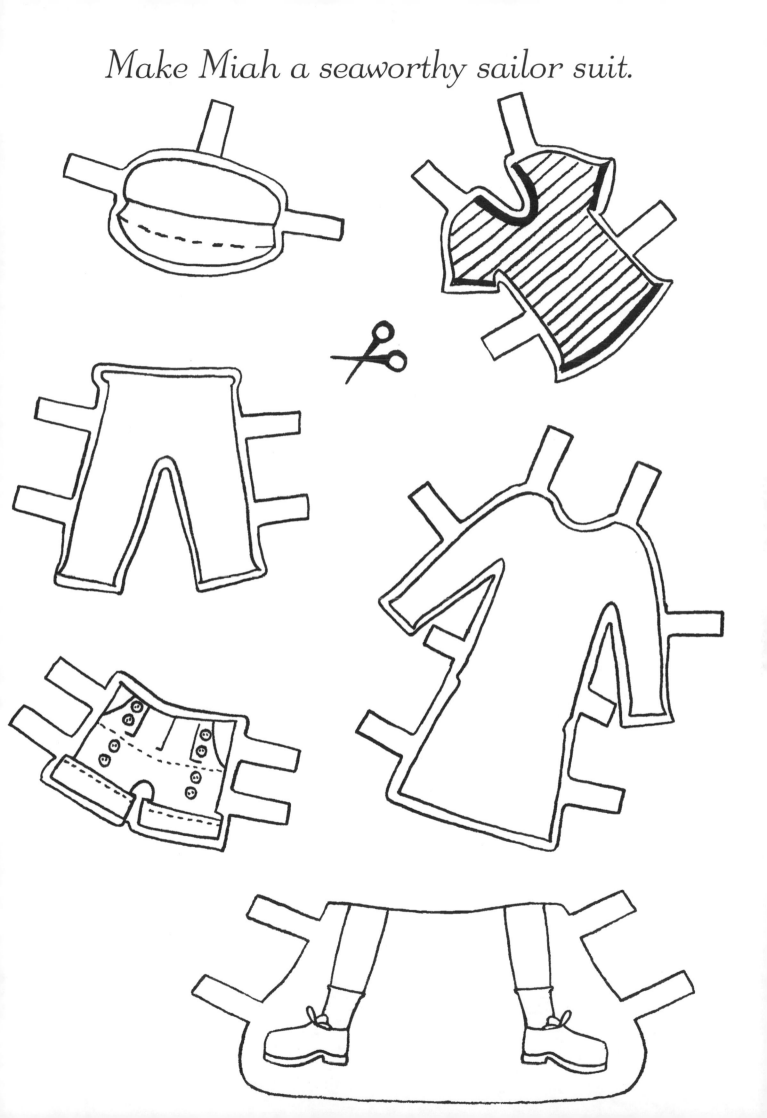

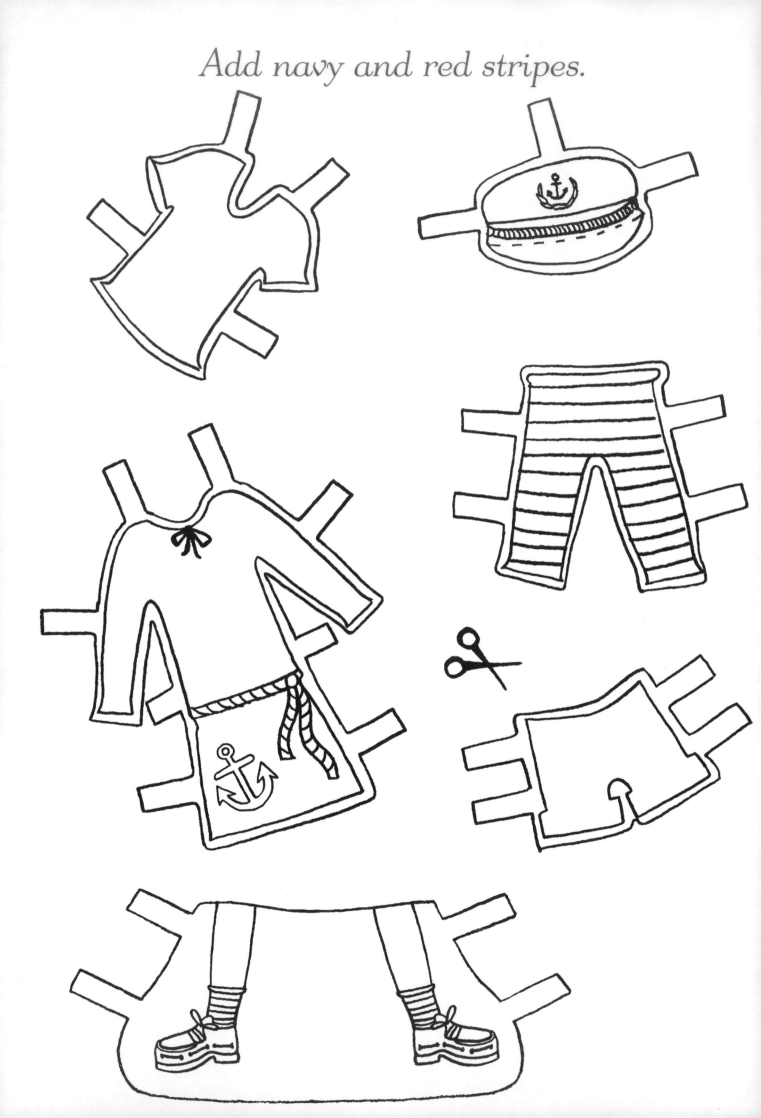

Add navy and red stripes.

Cherry will make a lovely bridesmaid.

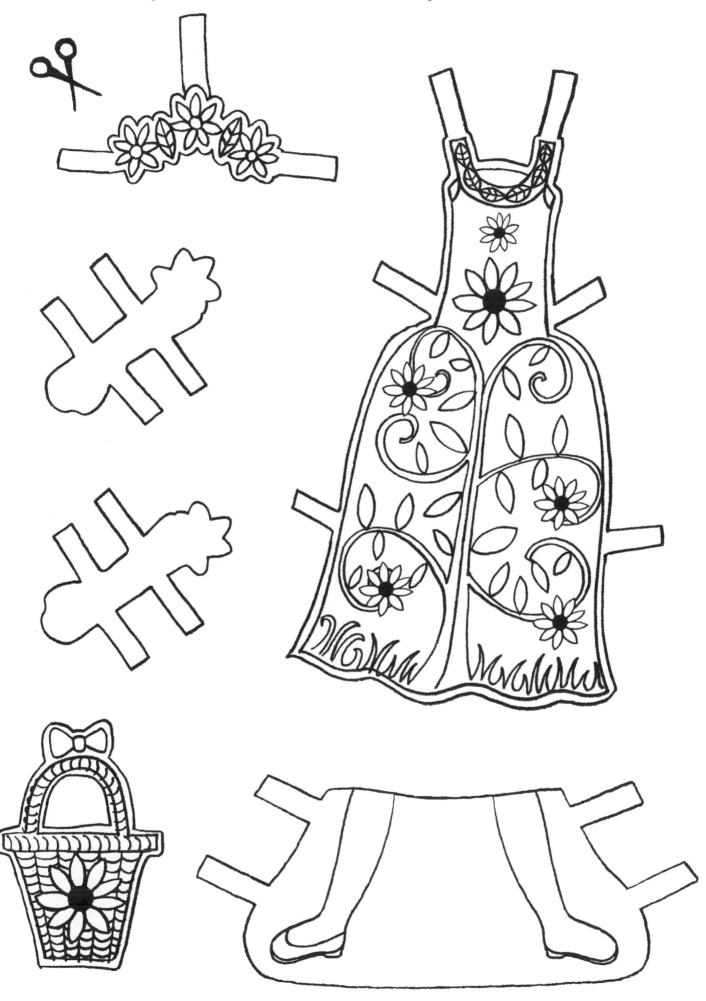

Decorate with bright petals.

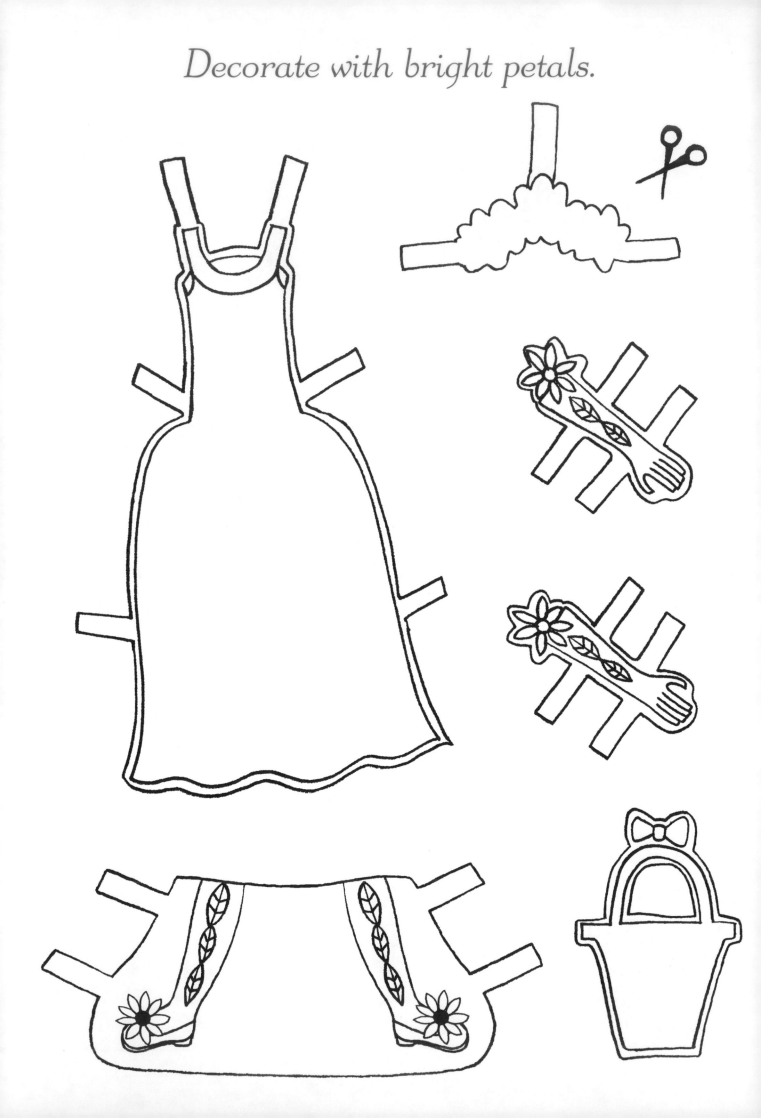

Doodle dolls love ribbons and bows.

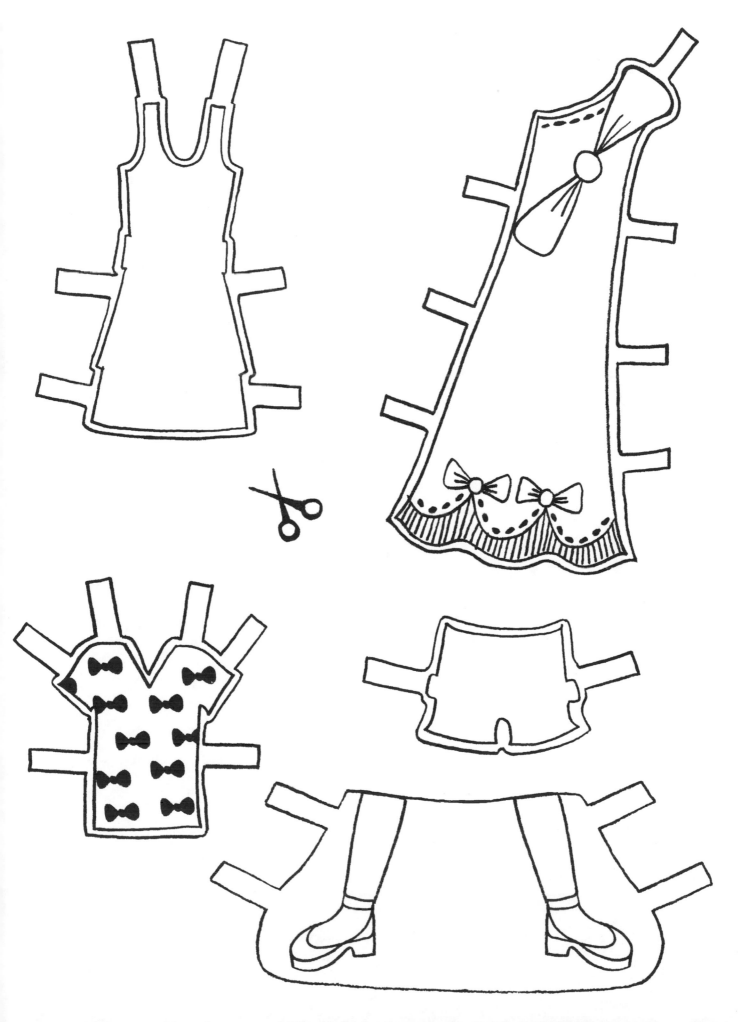

Pop a bow on every outfit.

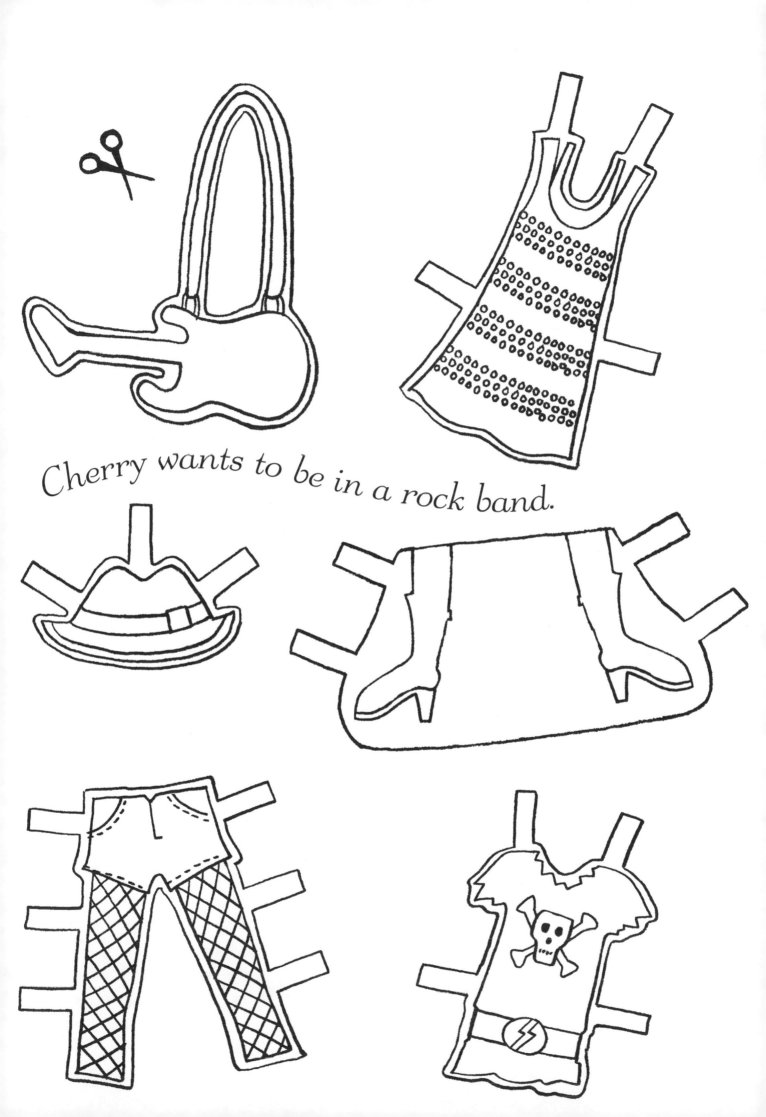

Cherry wants to be in a rock band.

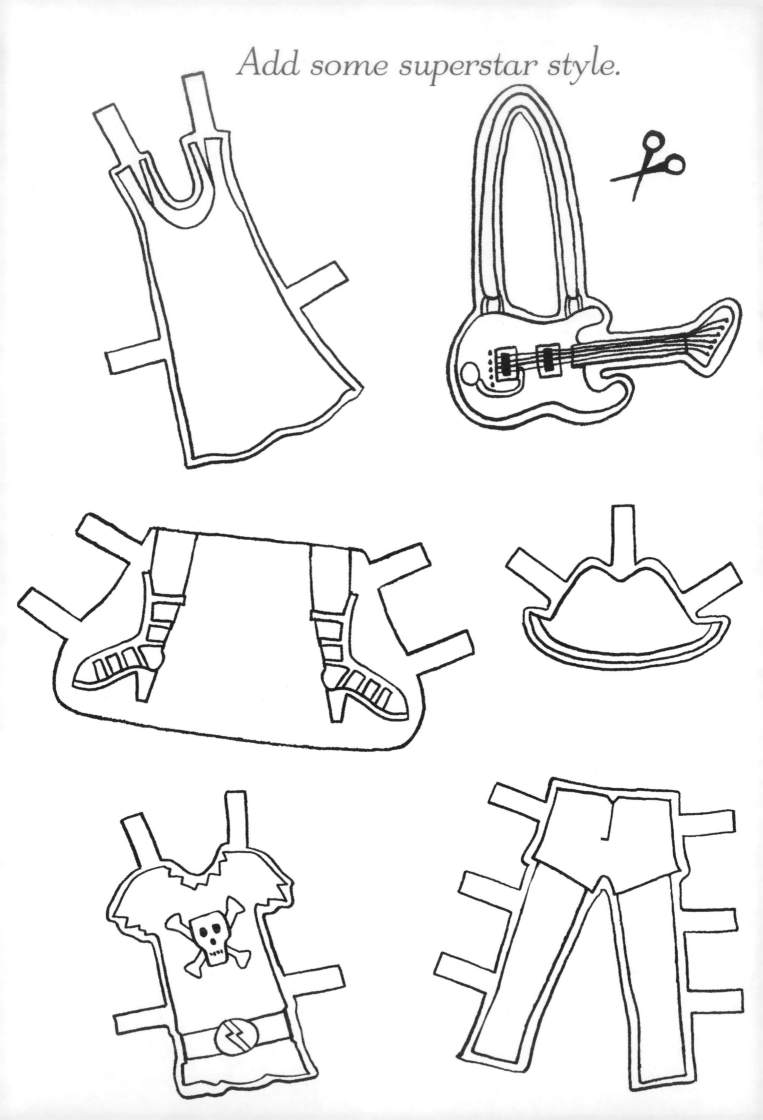

Add some superstar style.

Get the dolls ready for bed.

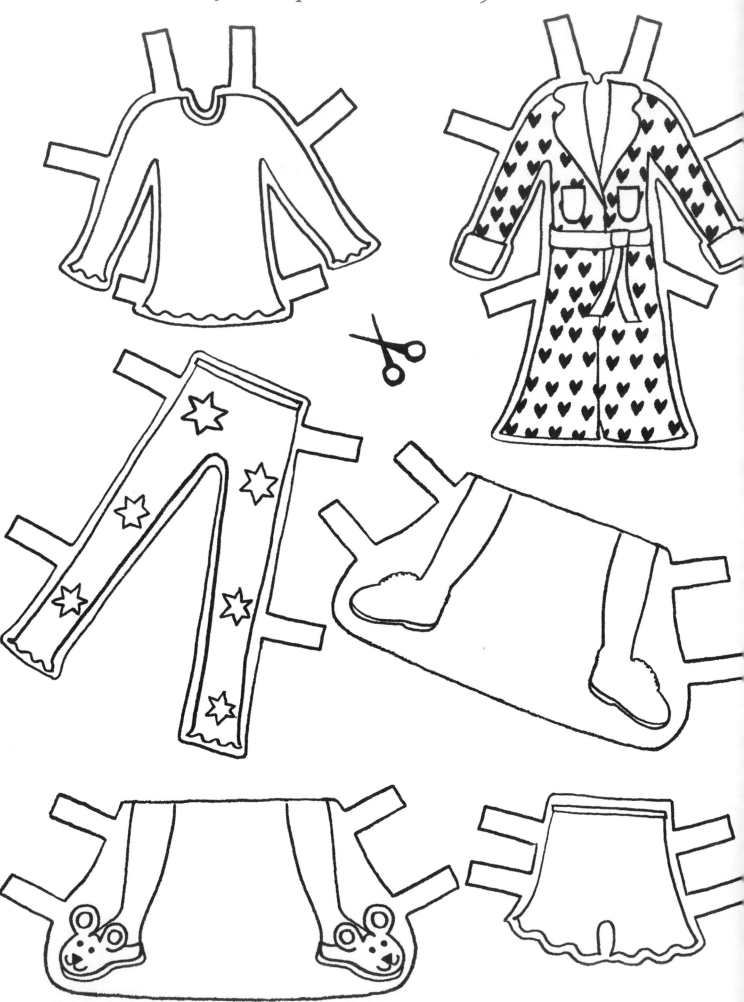

THE DOLLS CAN GO ANYWHERE

Draw Miah a pony.

Miah would go to a rodeo in America.

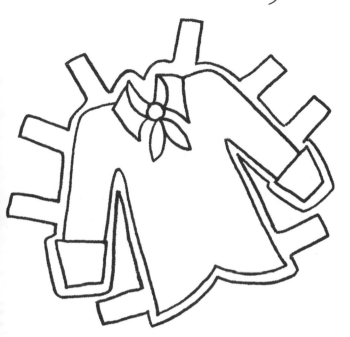

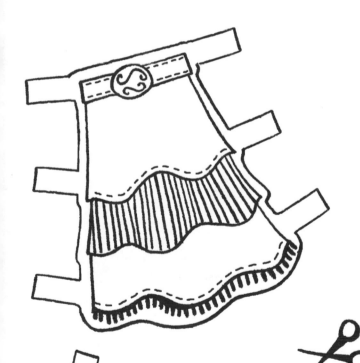

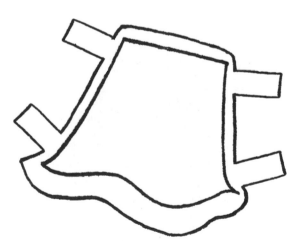

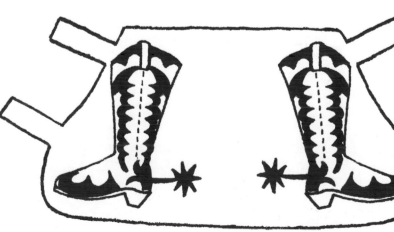

Yee-haw, cowgirl!

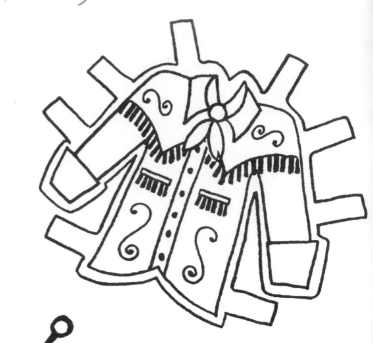

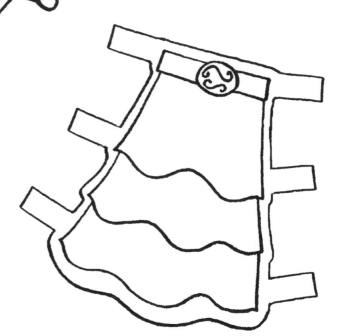

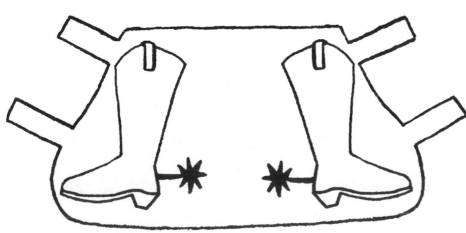

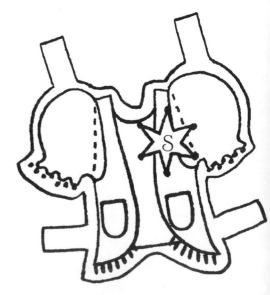

Cherry would wear tartan in Scotland.

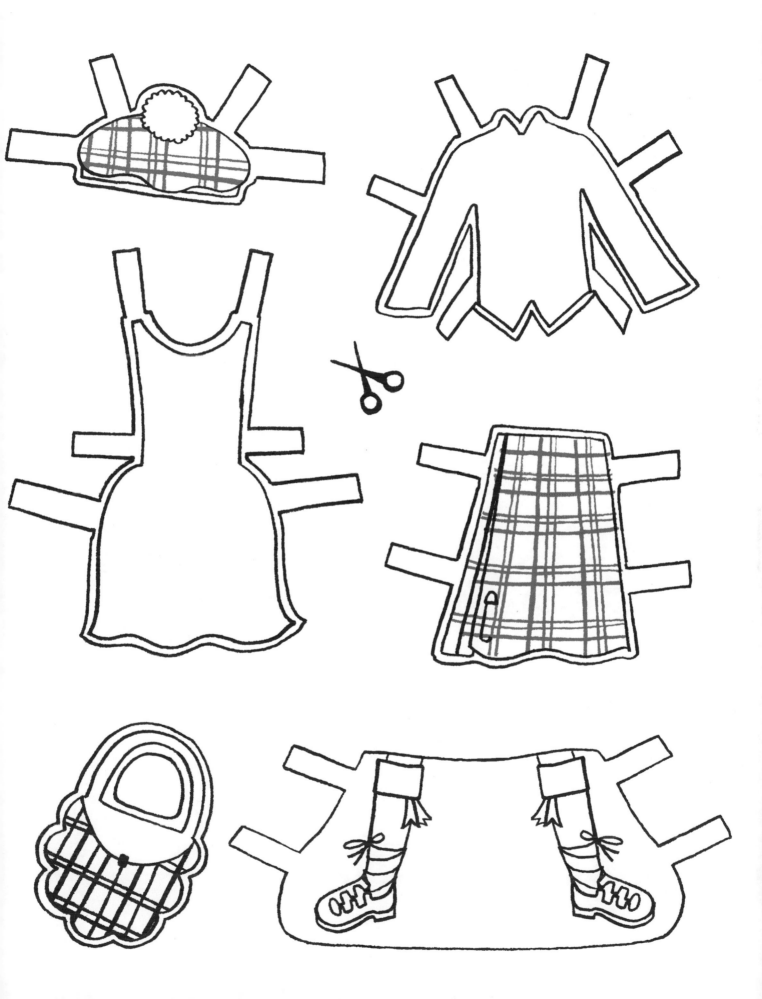

Add bold checks in red and green.

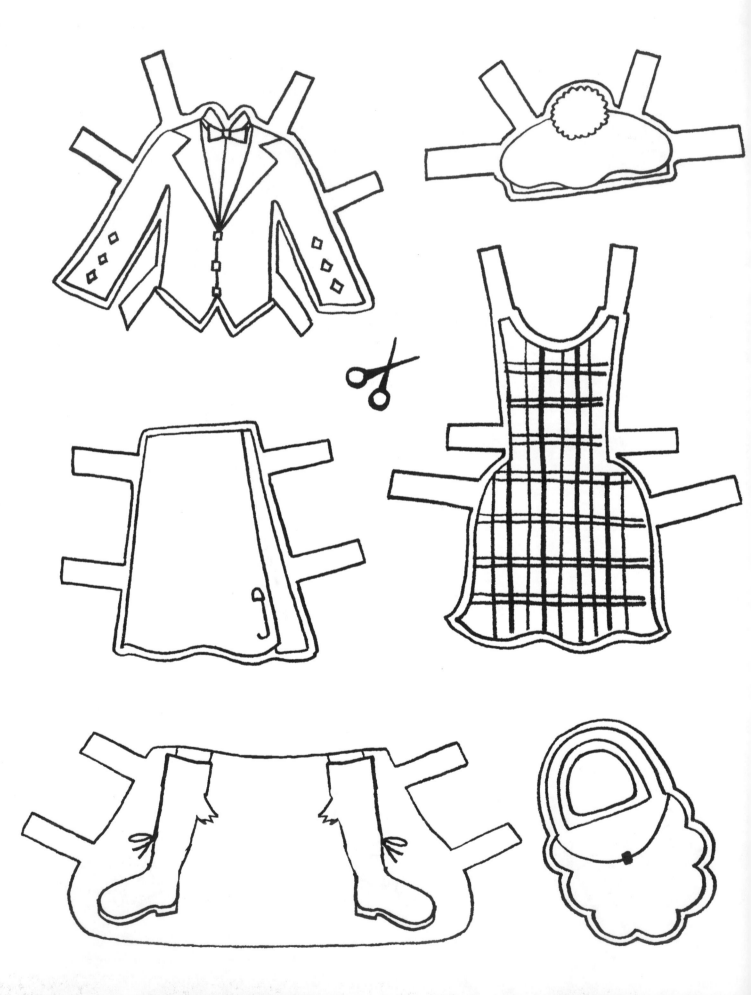

The dolls would love to fly to France.

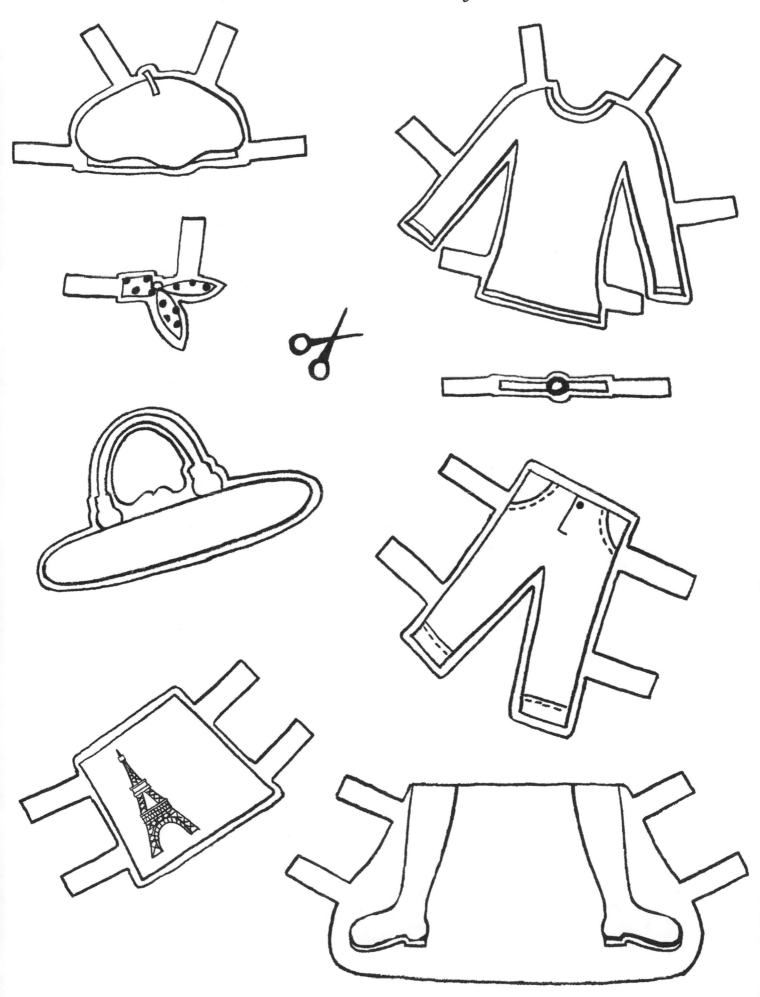

Complete with red, white, and blue.

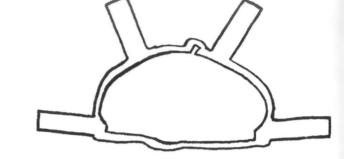

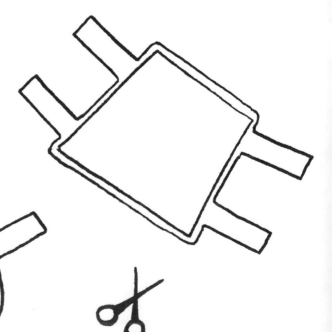

Miah might take a trip to Japan.

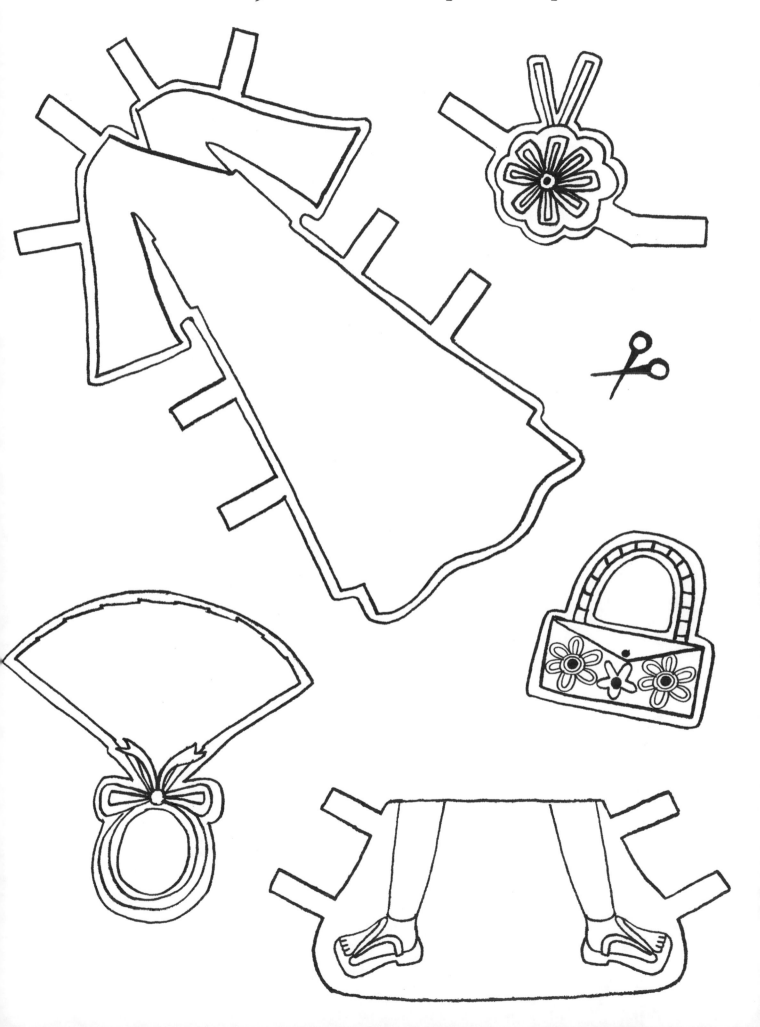

Add reds, greens, and purples to the kimono.

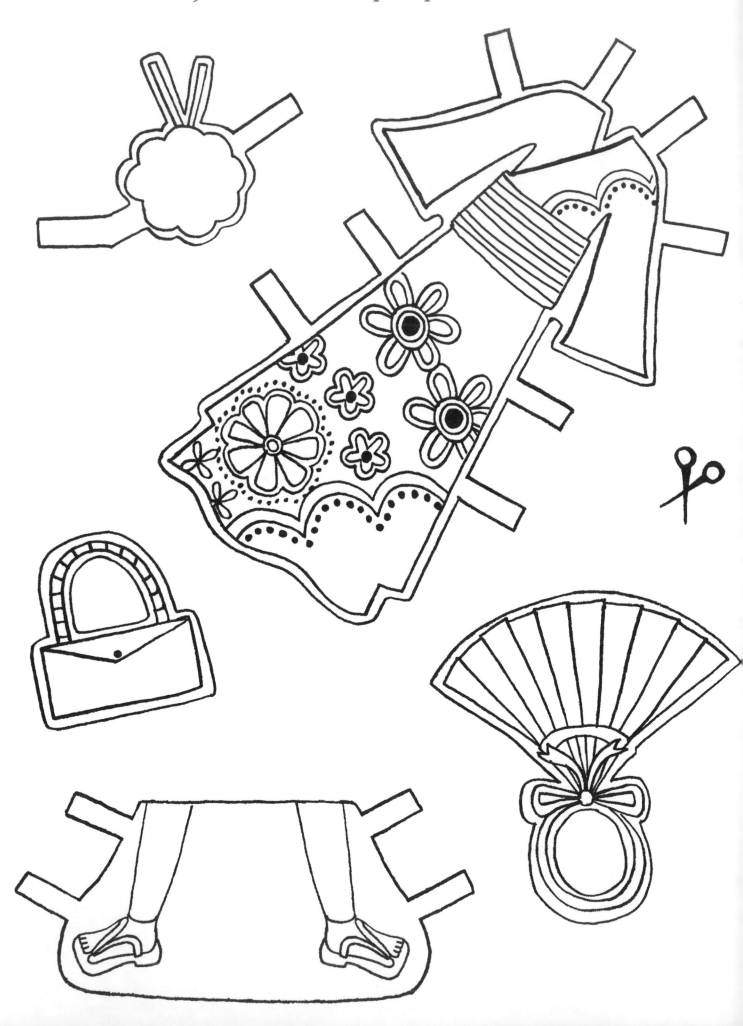

Cherry would dance at the carnival in Rio.

Make the costume look good enough to eat.

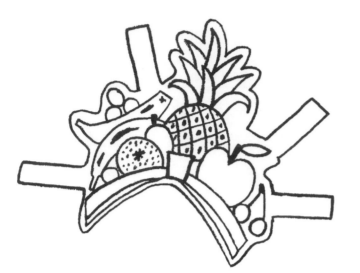

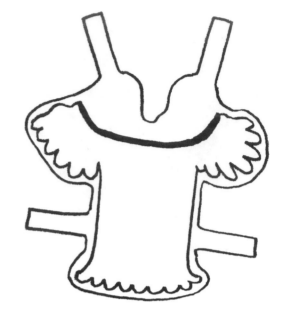

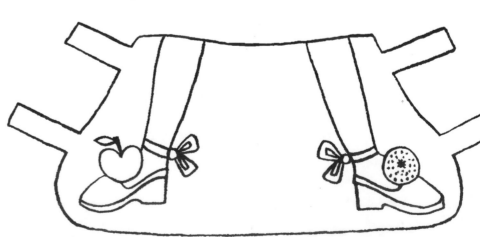

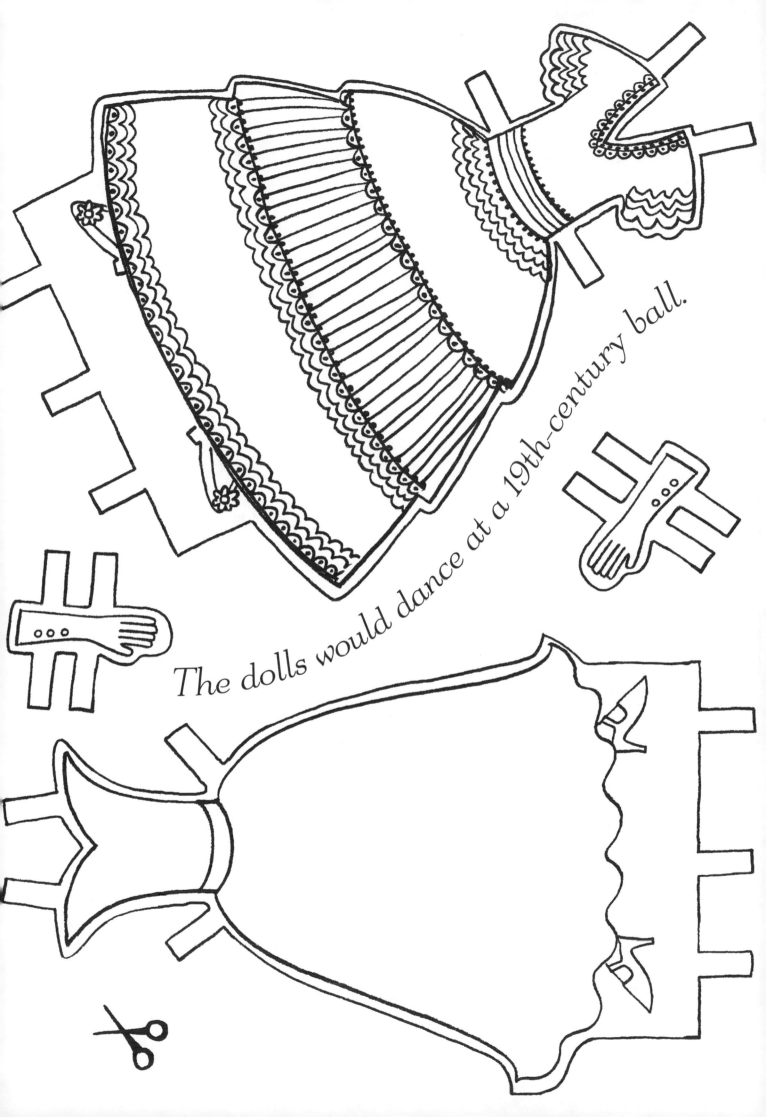

The dolls would dance at a 19th-century ball.

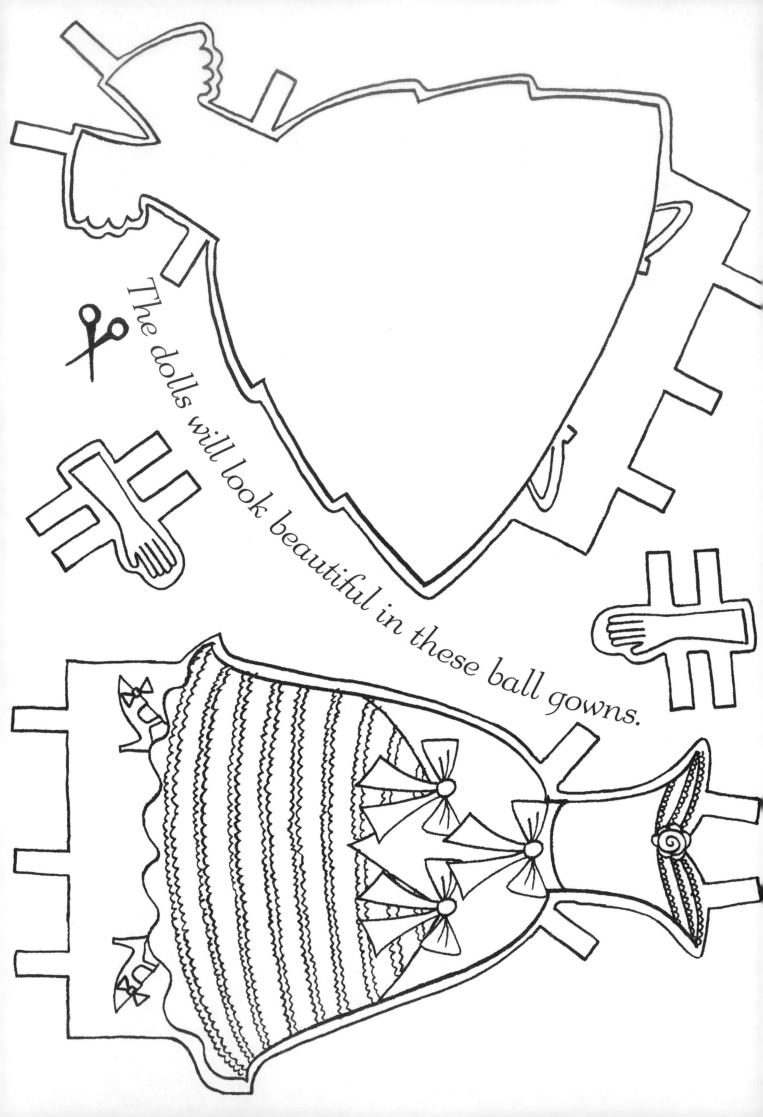

The dolls will look beautiful in these ball gowns.

They would enjoy an Edwardian tea party.

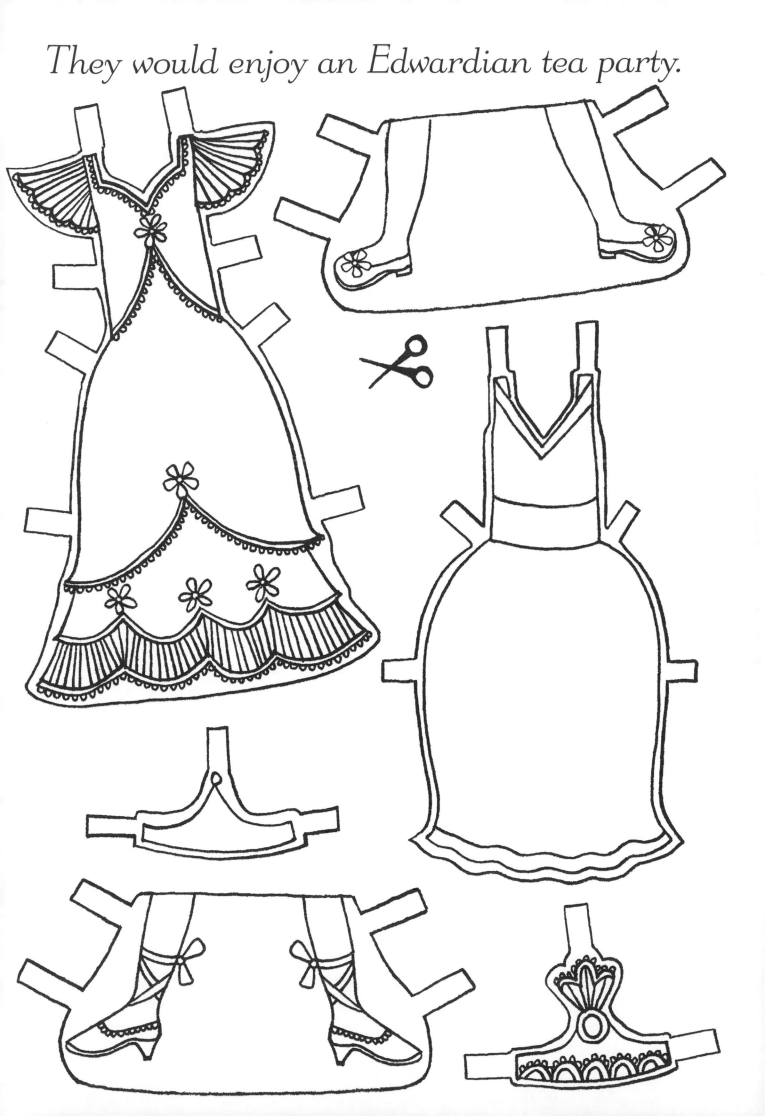

Decorate the frocks with flowers and frills.

Miah would dance all day in the 1920s.

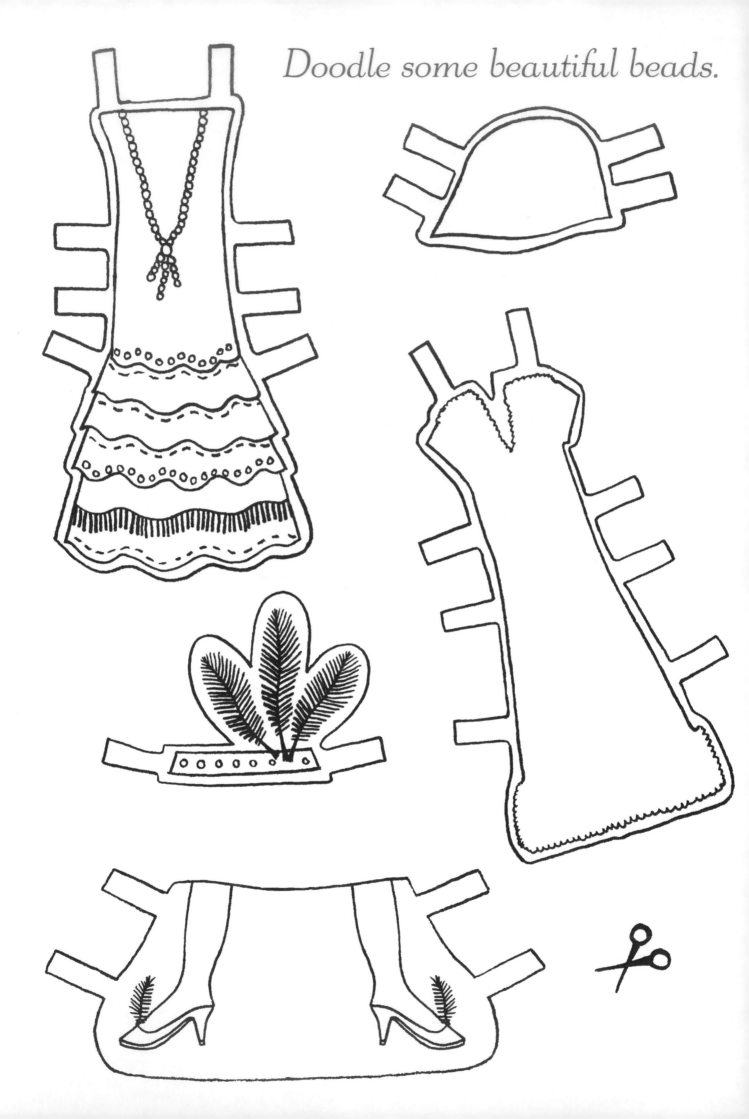

Doodle some beautiful beads.

Cherry would be a movie star in the 1950s.

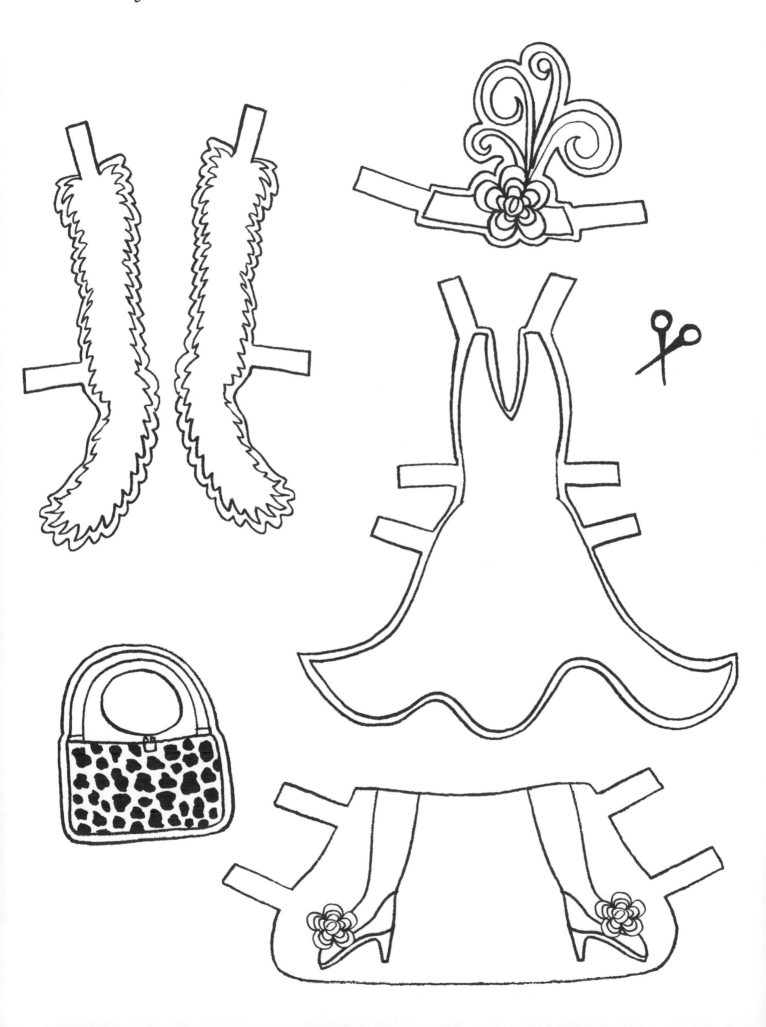

Add glamorous glitter and fabulous feathers.

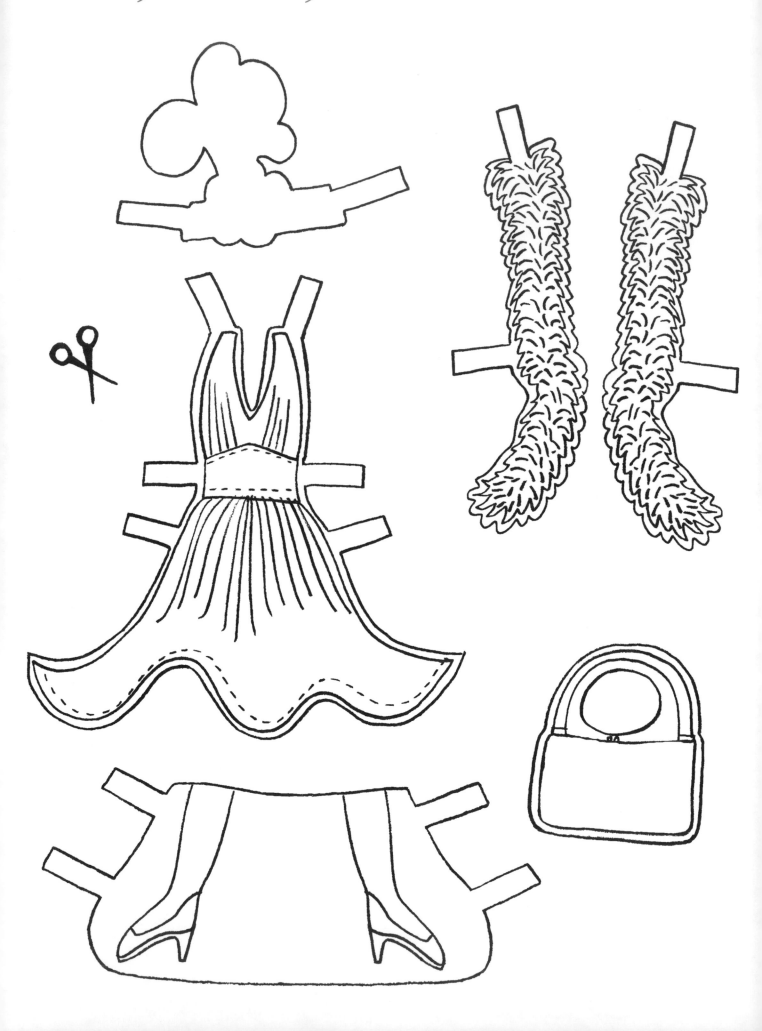

Make the dolls groovy in the 1960s...far out.

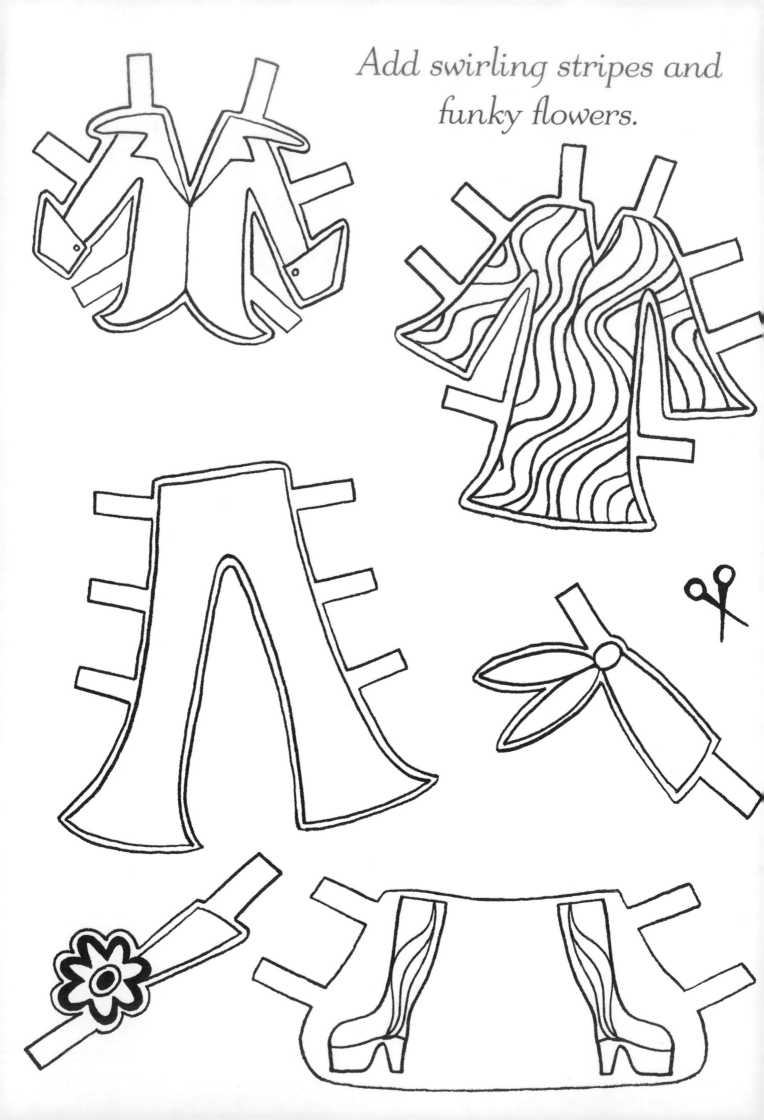

Add swirling stripes and funky flowers.

Miah might dance in a disco in the 1970s.

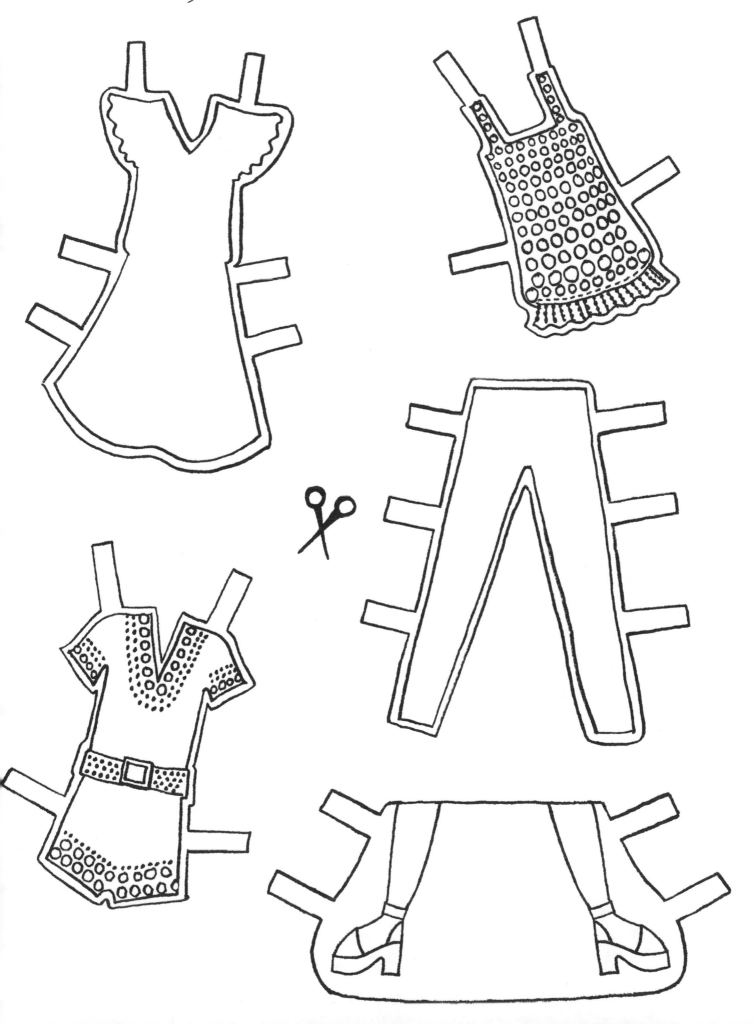

Add sequins and sparkles.

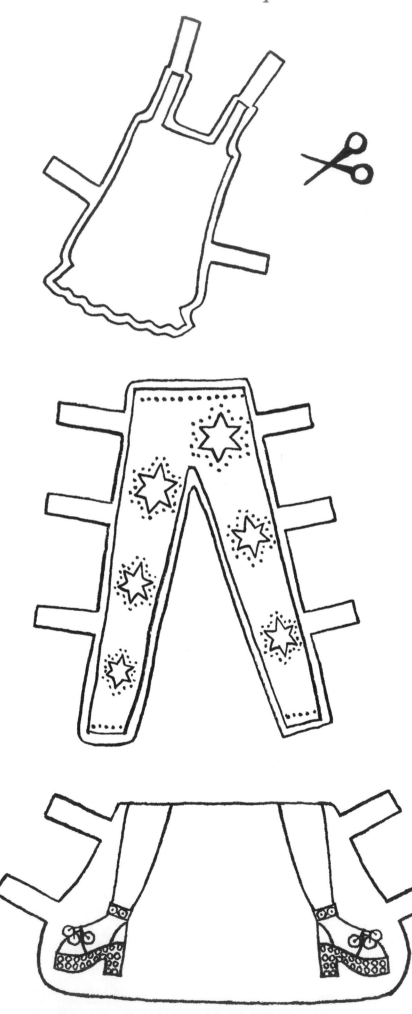
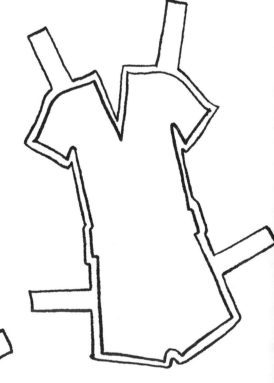
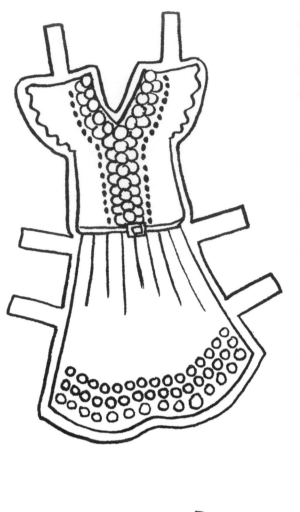

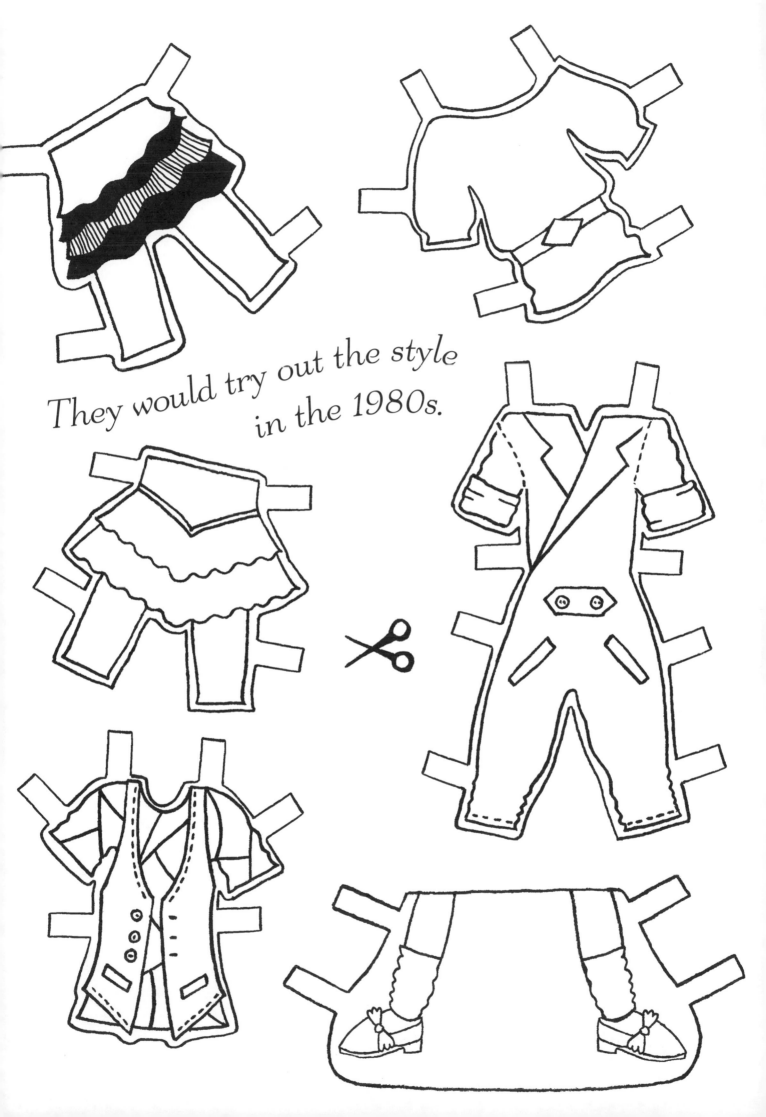

They would try out the style in the 1980s.

Add greens, yellows, reds, and blues.

DOODLE DOLLS
LOVE COSTUMES

What is Cherry juggling?

Cherry would love to be a clown.

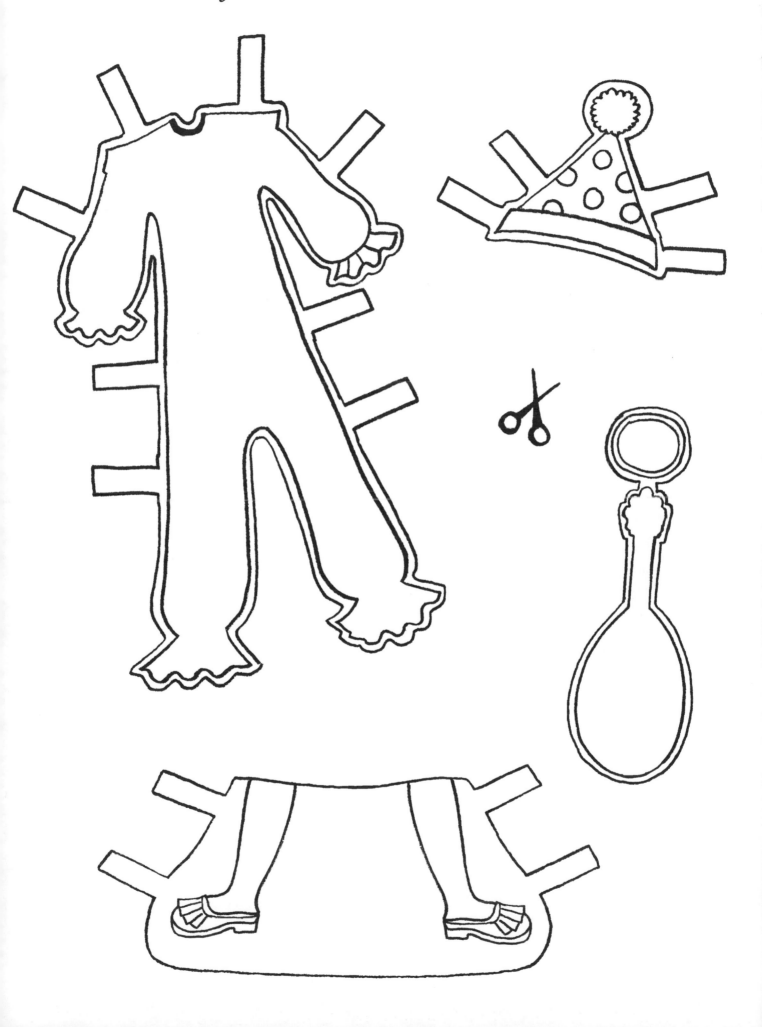

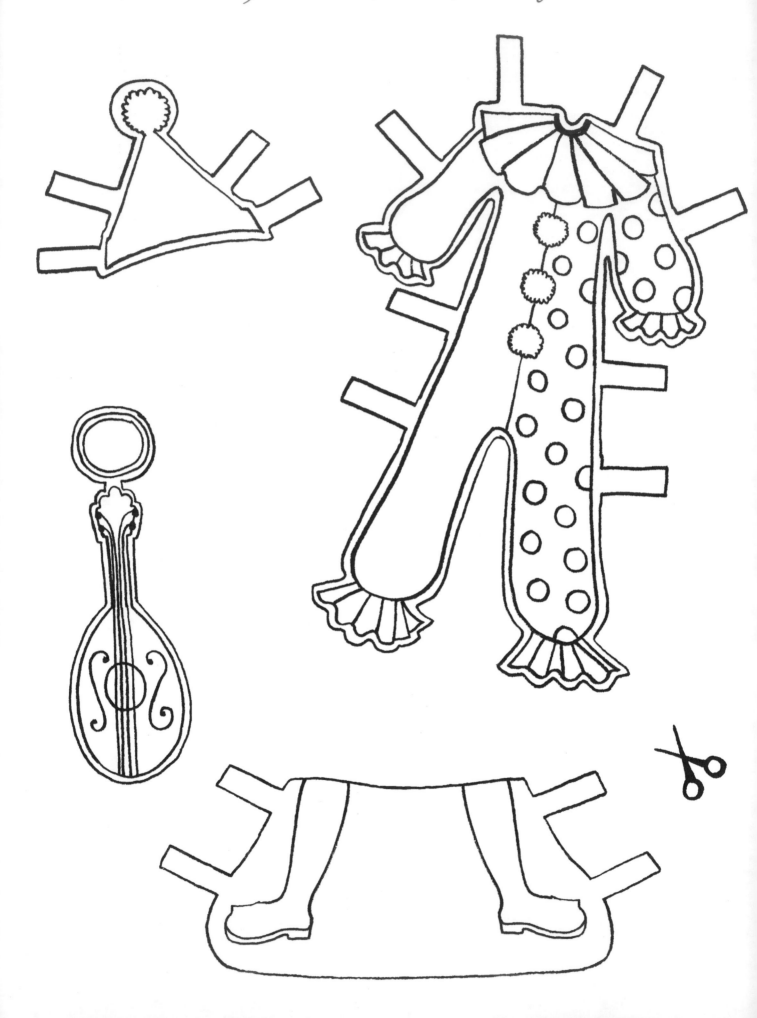

The Wardrobe.

Fold here

Lock

Fold here

Lock

C   Glue here

B   Glue here

Slot

Slot

Miah would be a jolly jester.

Red, green, and yellow will be perfect.

Dress Cherry like a mermaid.

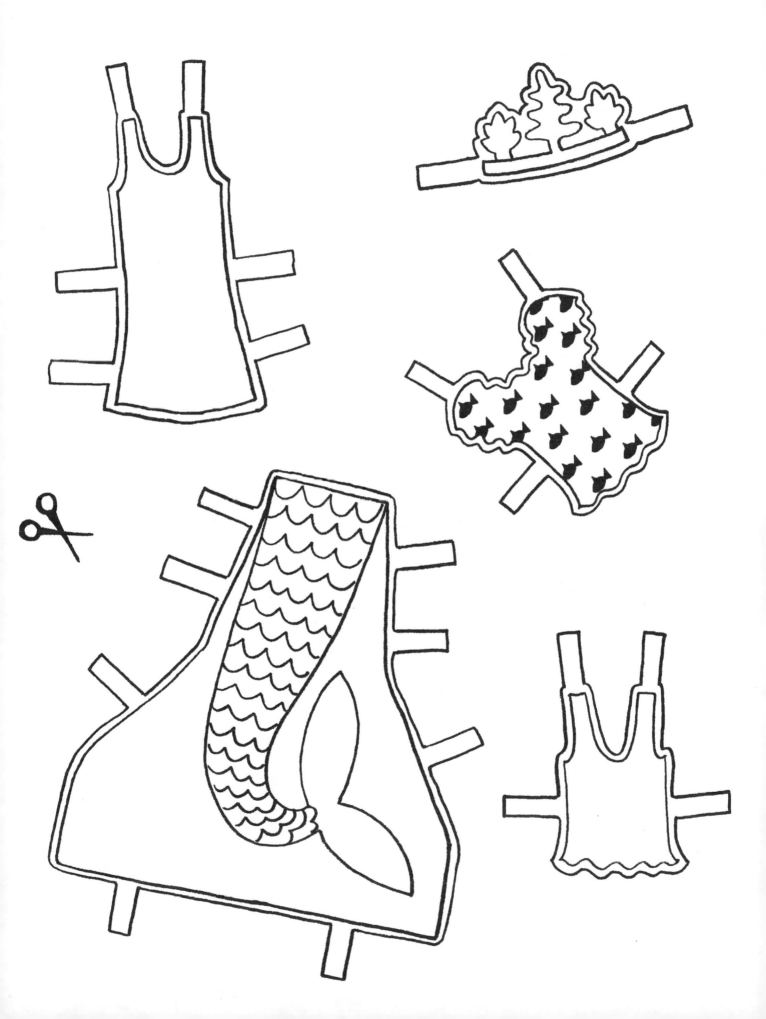

Finish the fishy tail, and add lots of shells.

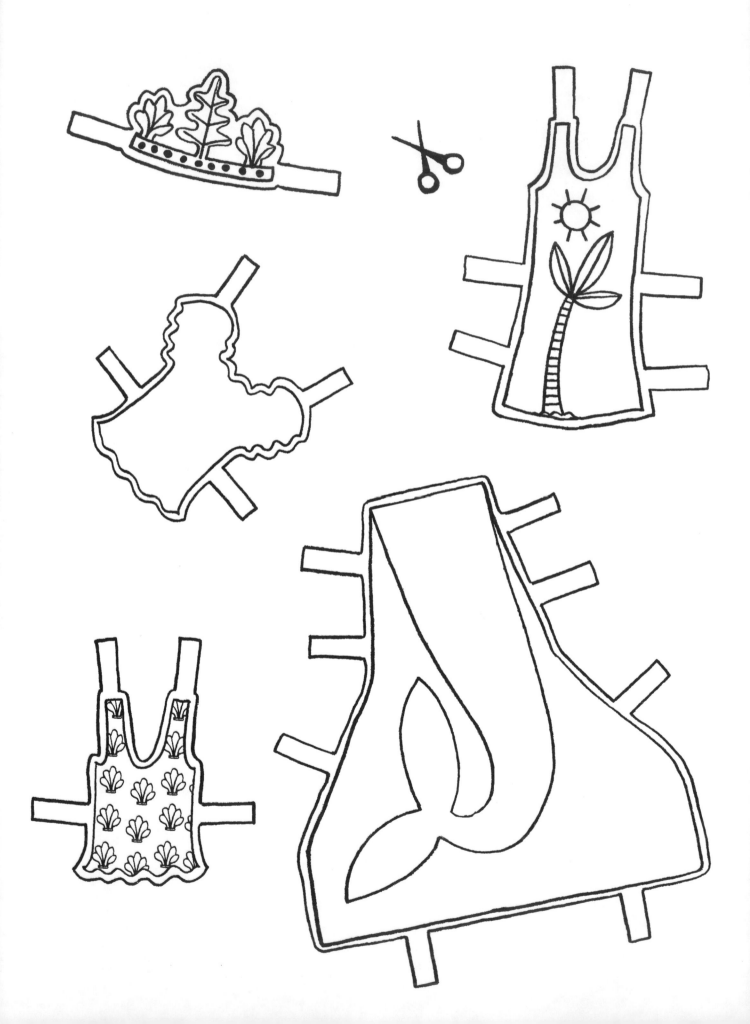

Could the doodle dolls be bugs?

Finish the buzzy bee and lovely ladybug.

Make Miah into a beautiful butterfly.

Add patterns and bright colors.

Disguise Miah for a masked ball.

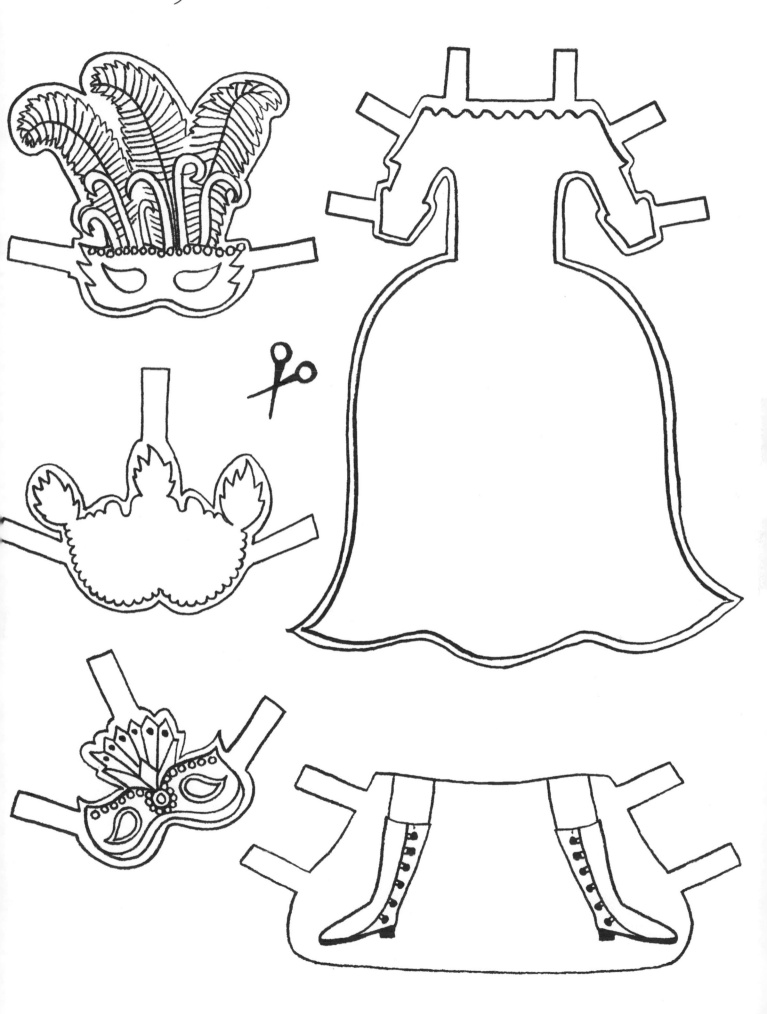

Finish the feathers and add lots of color.

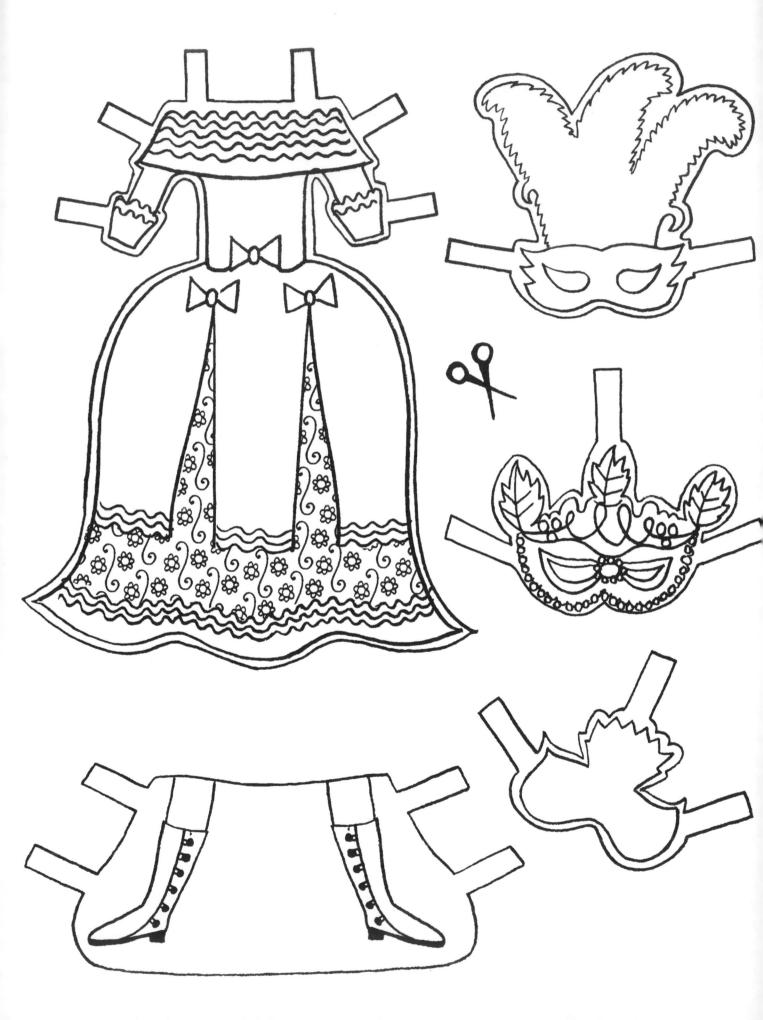

Who wants to be Cinderella?

Make sure Cinderella can go to the ball.

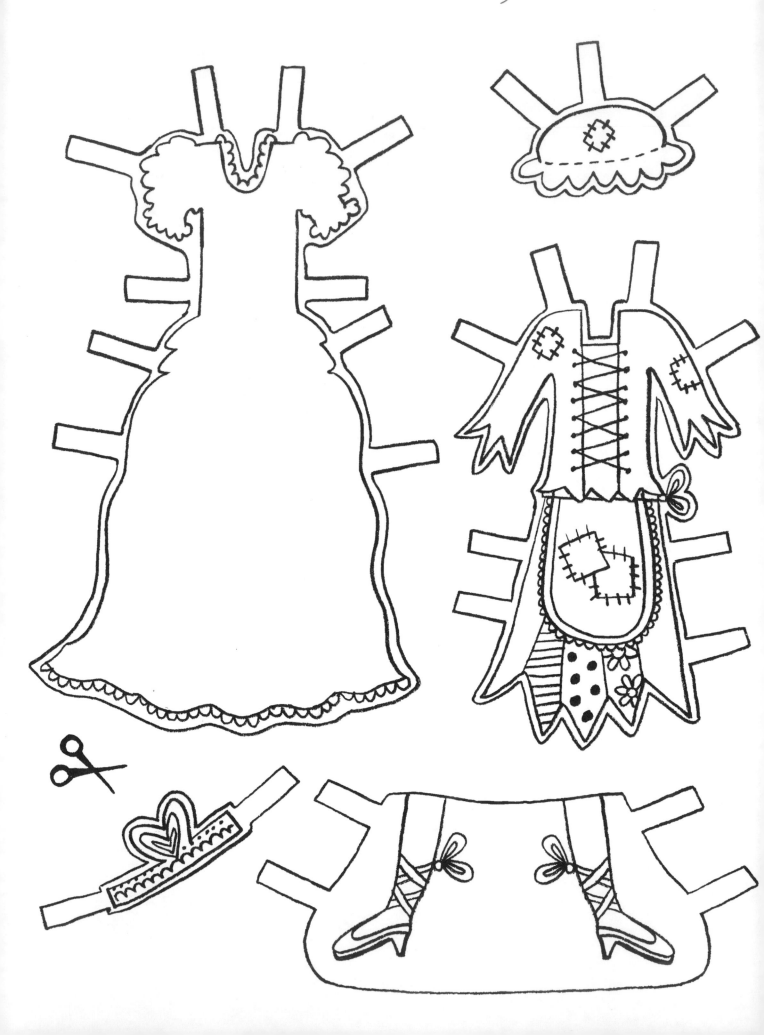

Dress Cherry like a cherry cupcake.

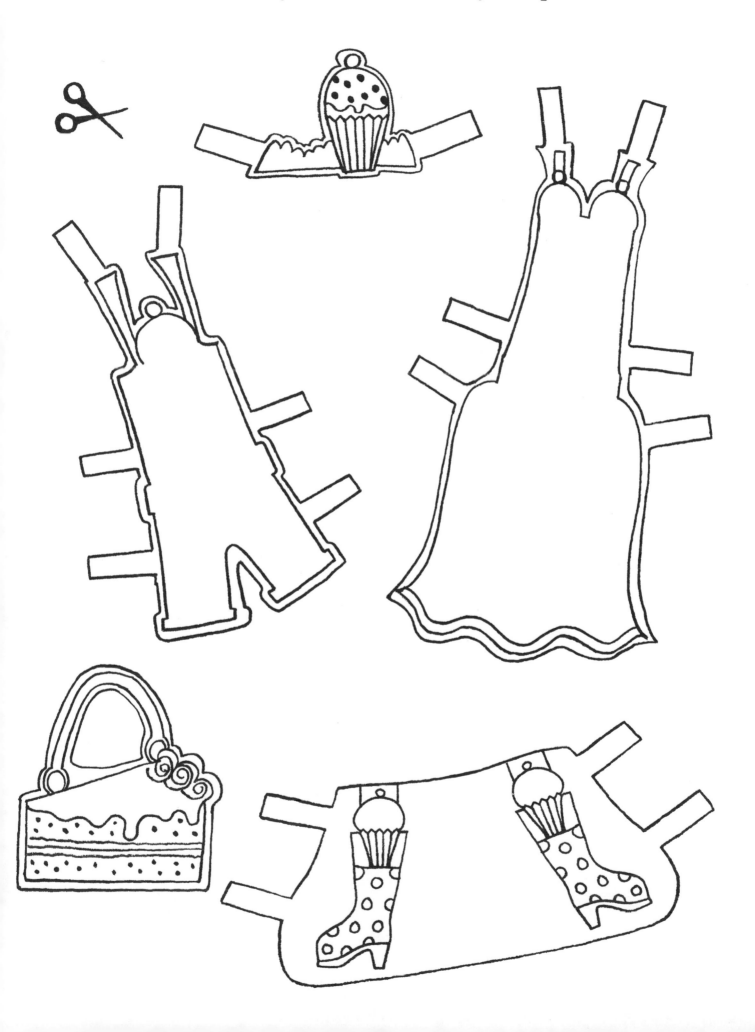

Add cherries and plenty of icing.

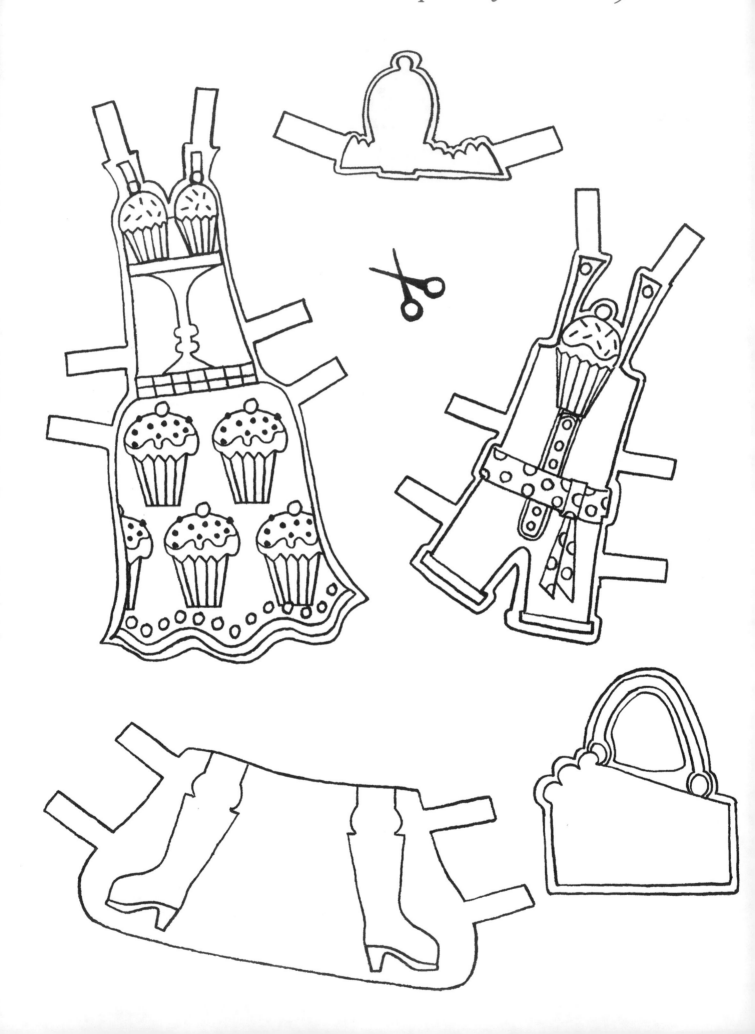

Doodle dolls like to play hospital.

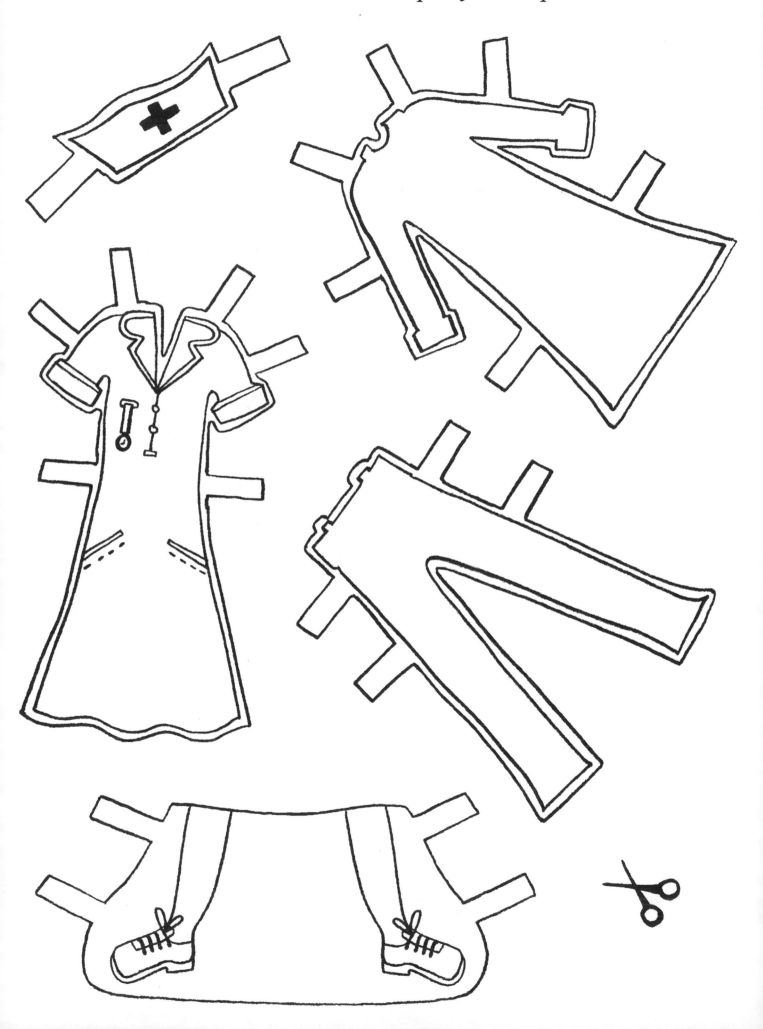

Make them ready for the patients.

Miah might be a chef.

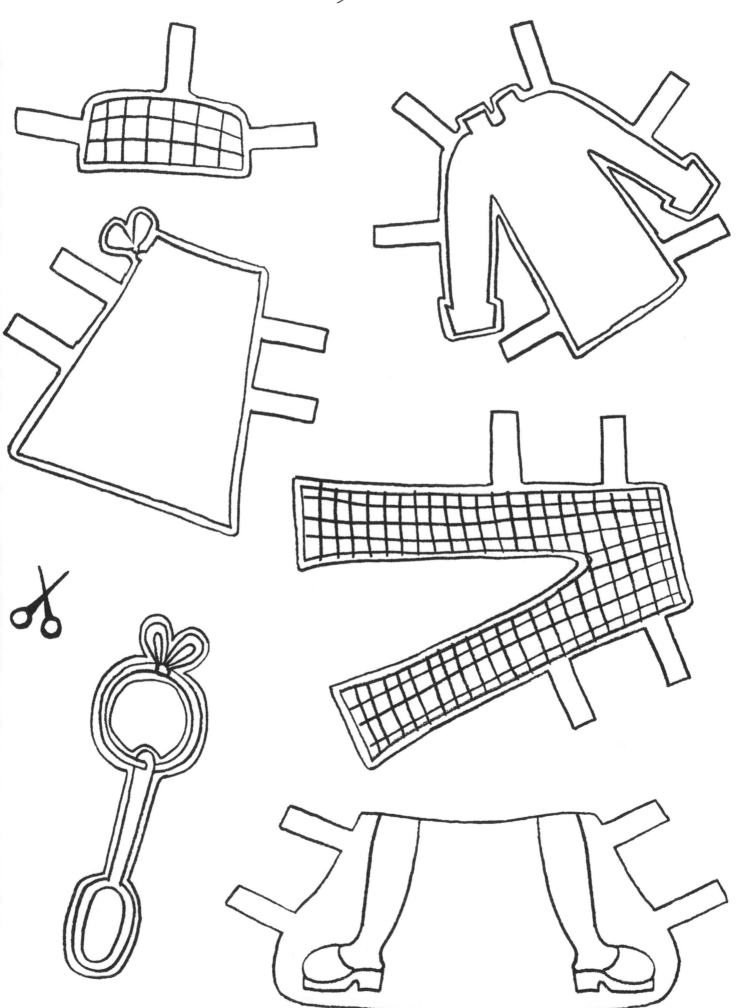

Finish the outfit with checks and buttons.

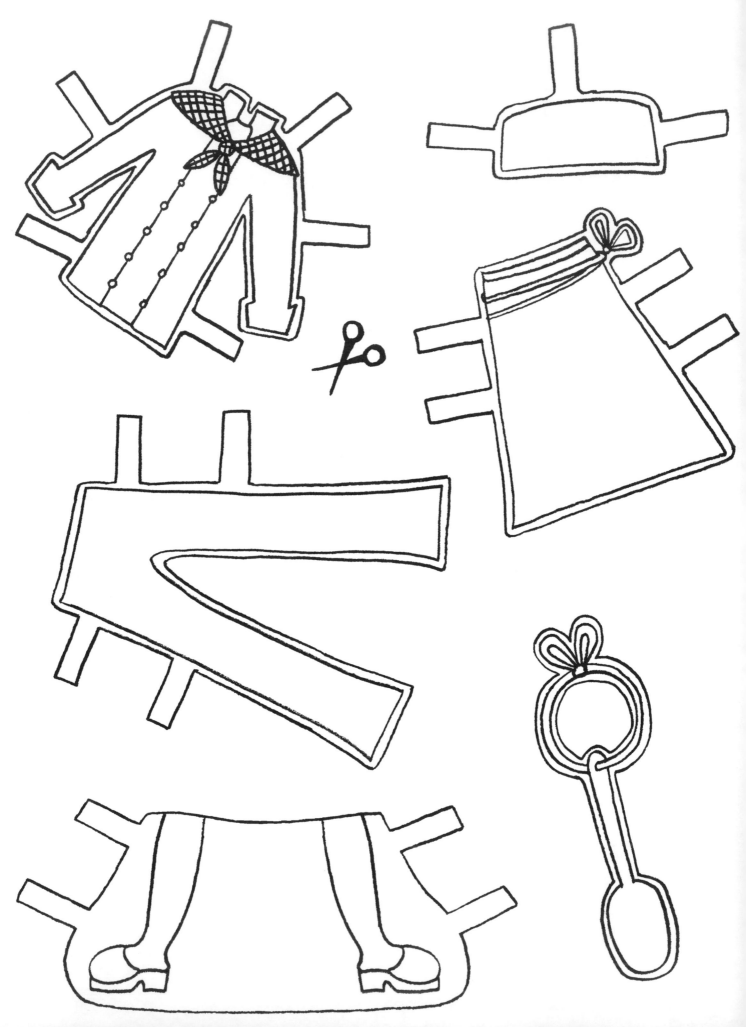

Who would sail the seas as a pirate?

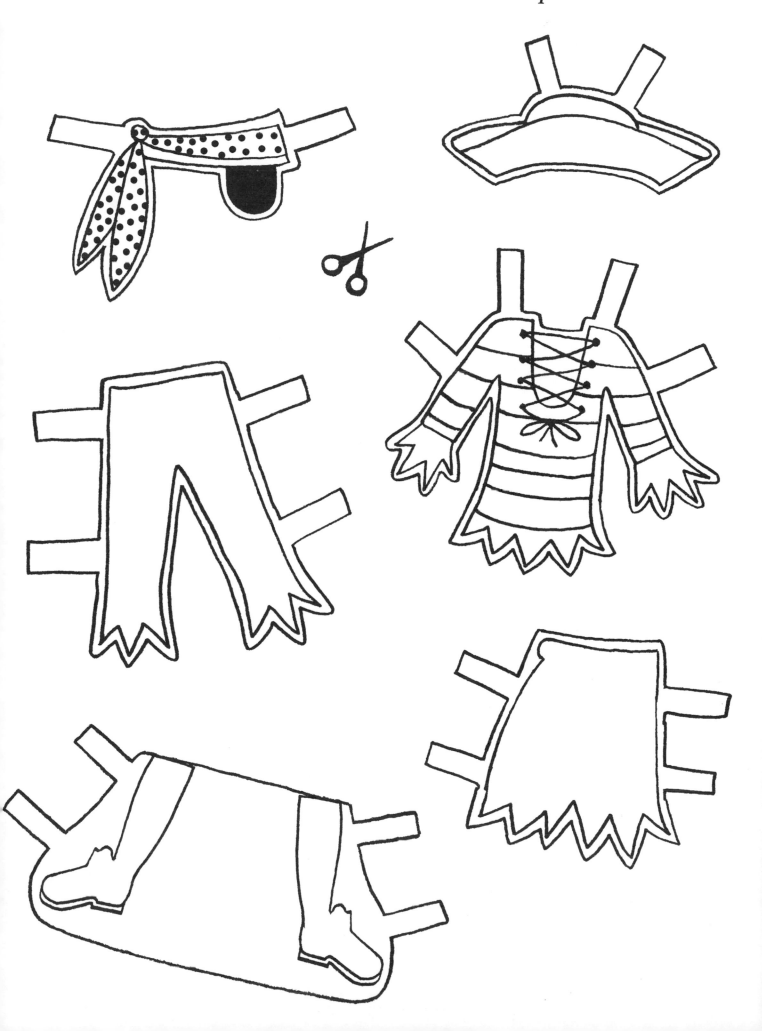

Ship ahoy!

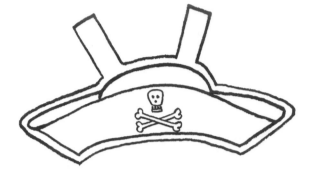

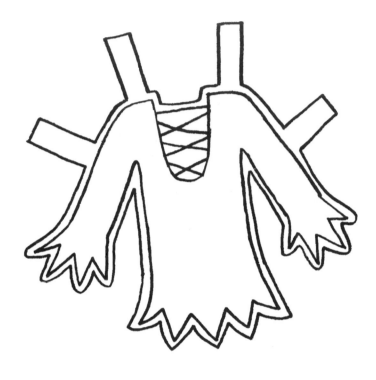

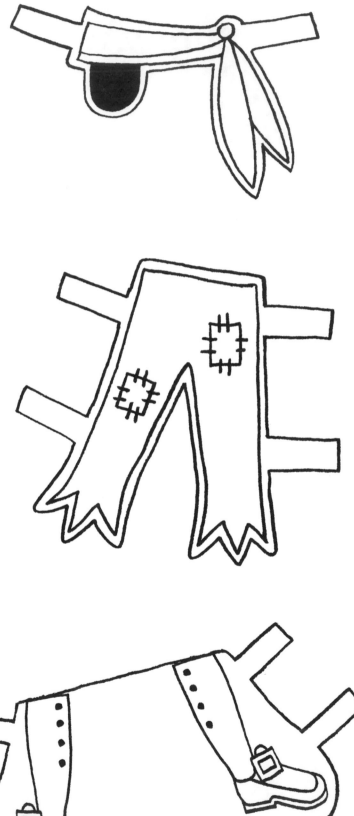

Cherry would love to be Little Bo Peep.

Add pretty pinks and pale blues.

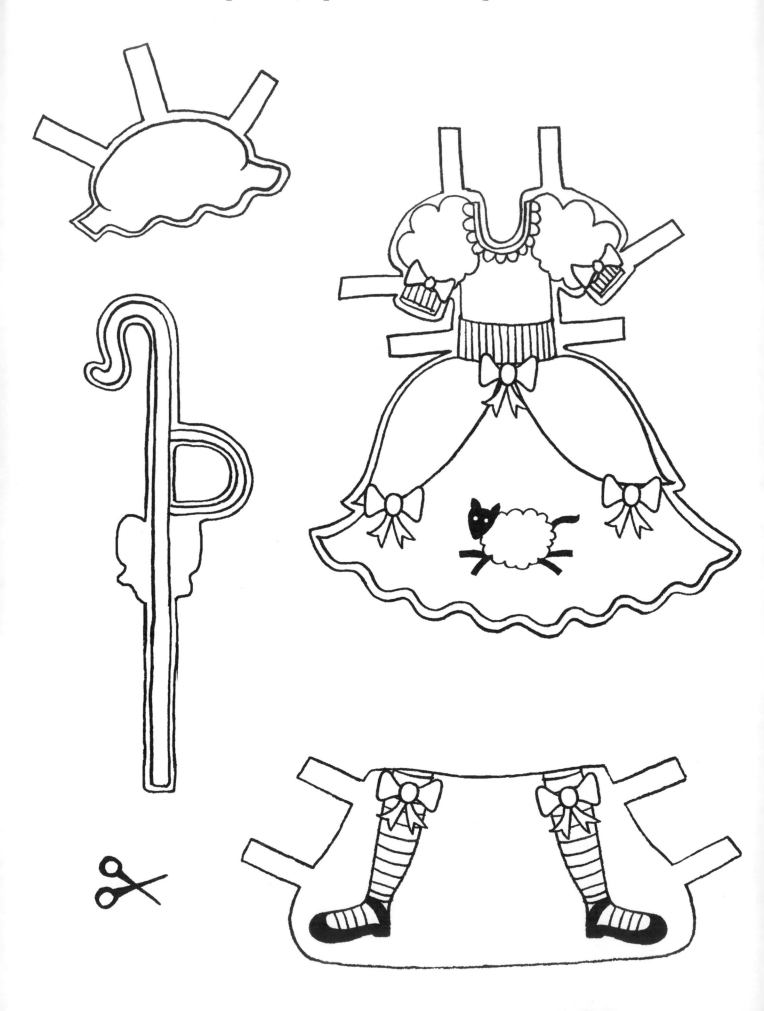

Miah would be Little Red Riding Hood.

What a nice outfit for visiting Grandma's house.

Make Miah into a math-magician.

A cool calculator bag and numbered dresses.

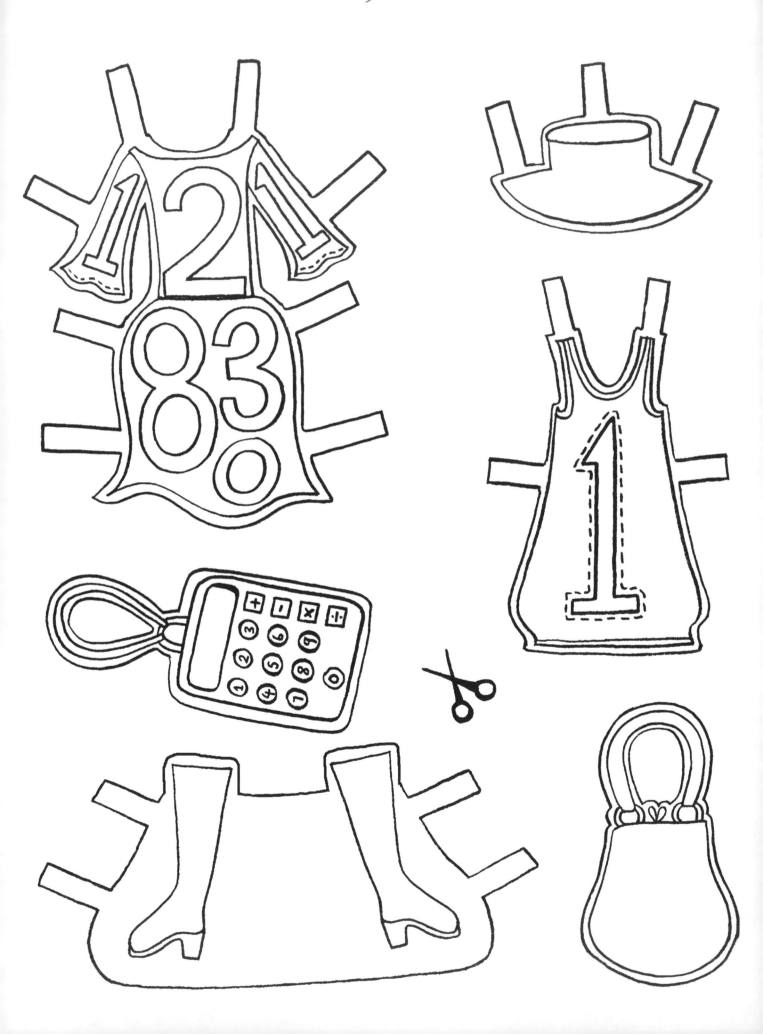

Who is the prettiest doll in the pack?

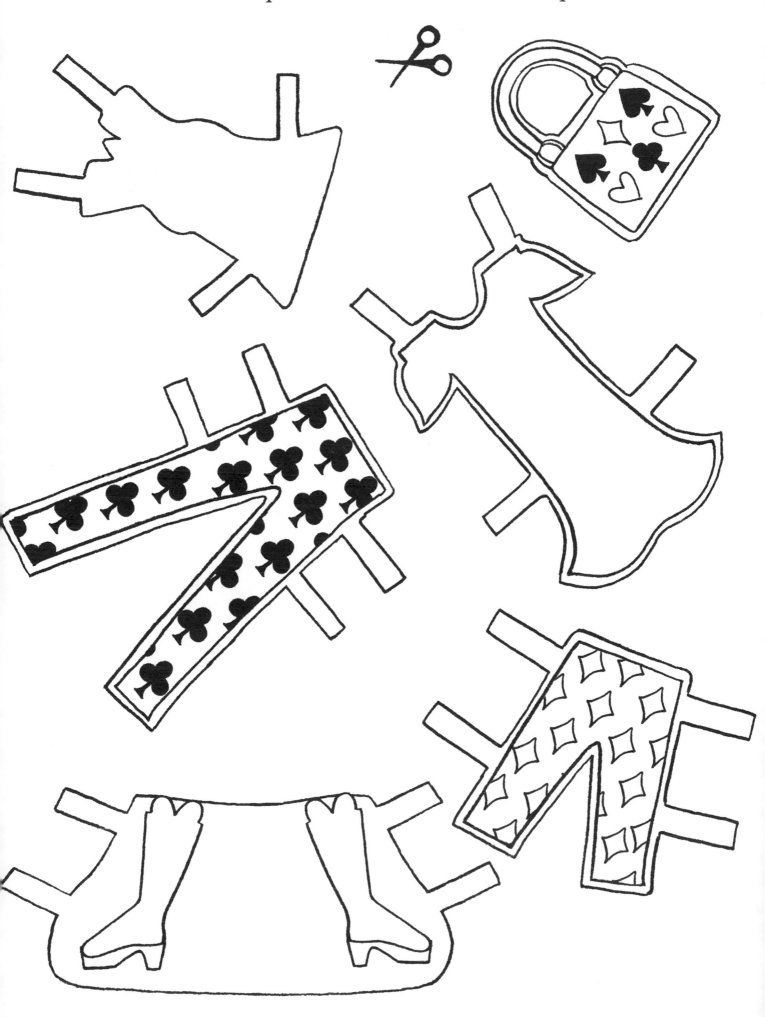

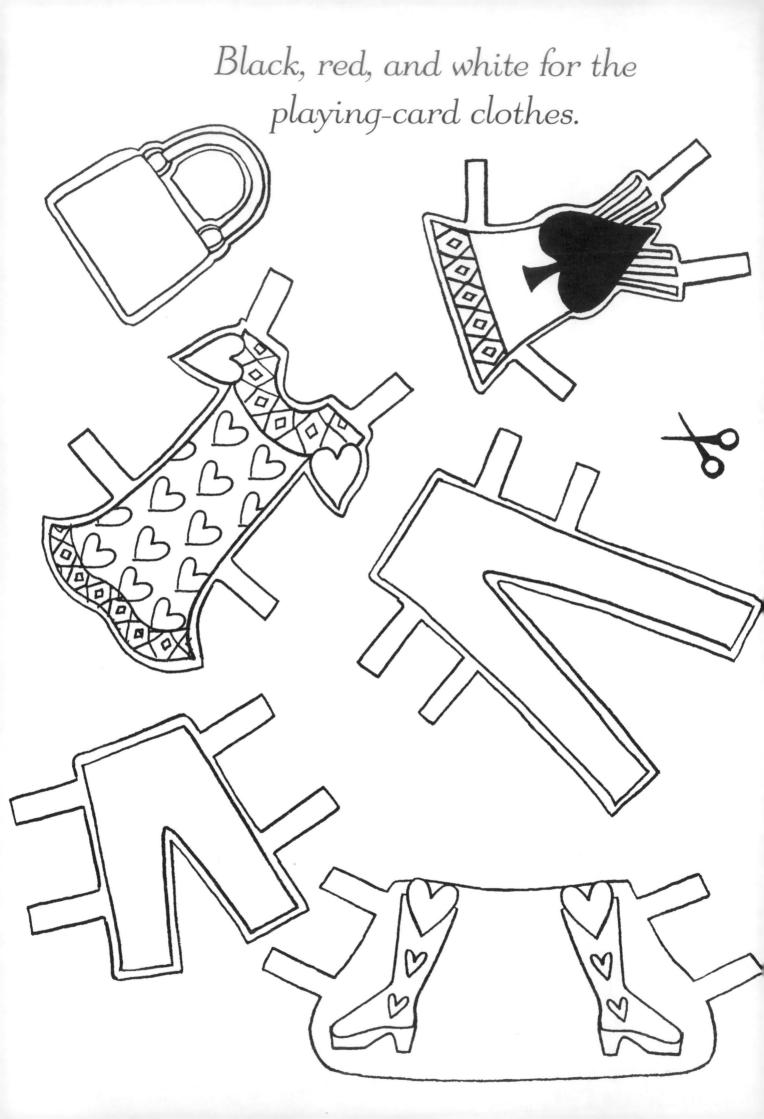

Black, red, and white for the playing-card clothes.

Cherry is a super girl.

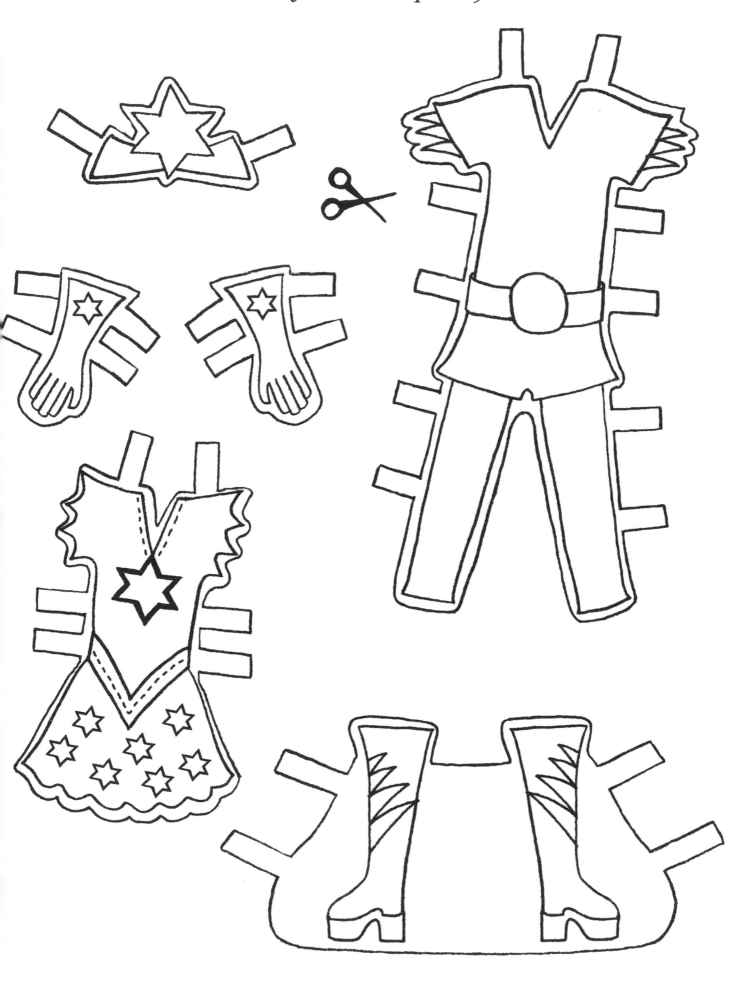

Save the day in super stars and stripes.

Create a cute cat costume.

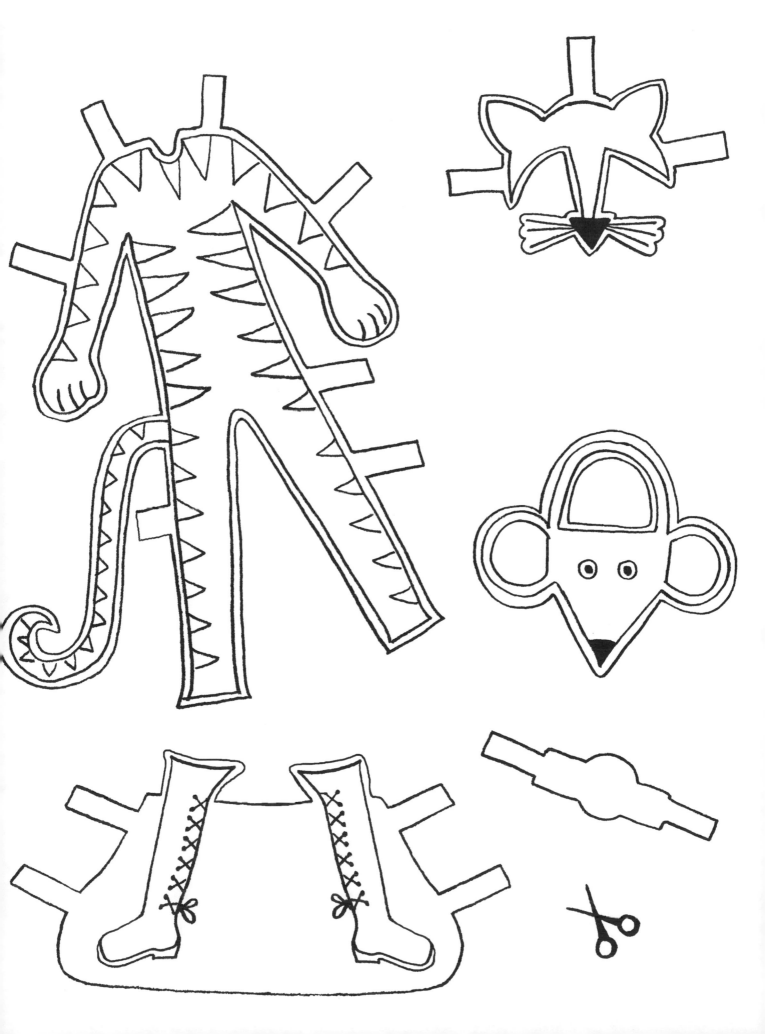

Add some "purr"-fect stripes.

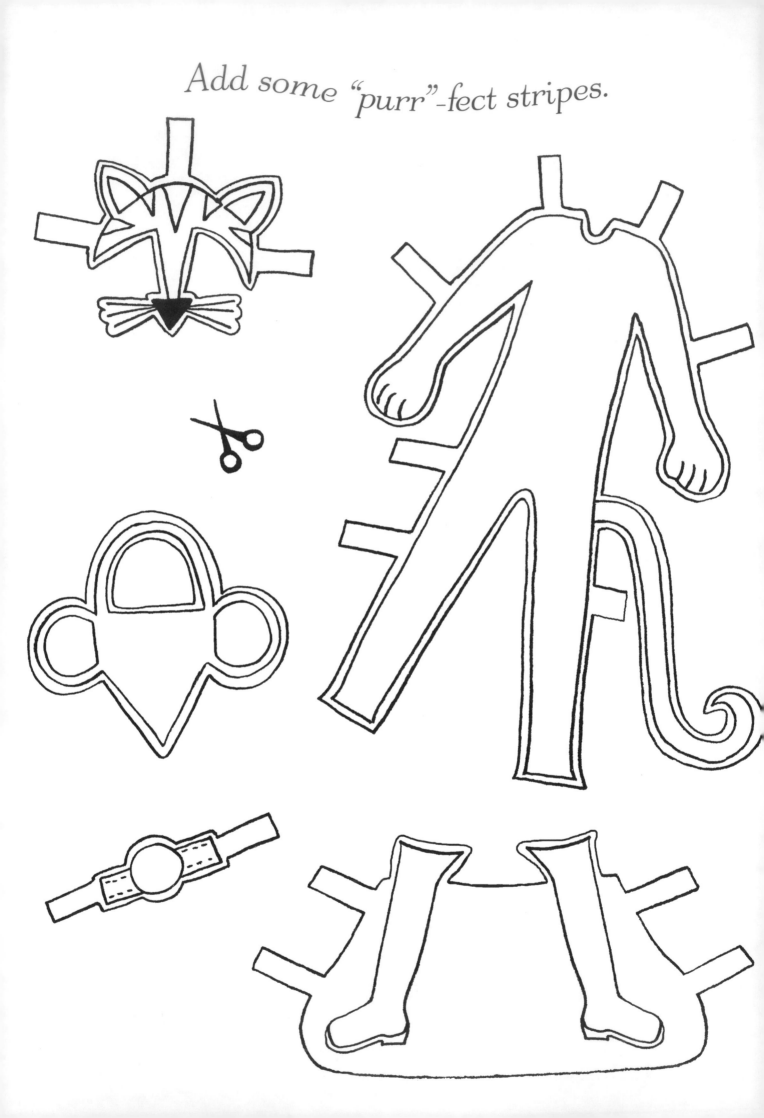

Now make a marvelous mouse suit.

Fluffy fur and a pink tail will be perfect.

DOODLE DOLLS
LOVE HAVING FUN

Finish Miah's skating outfit.

Cherry practices ballet.

Miah loves to skate for hours.

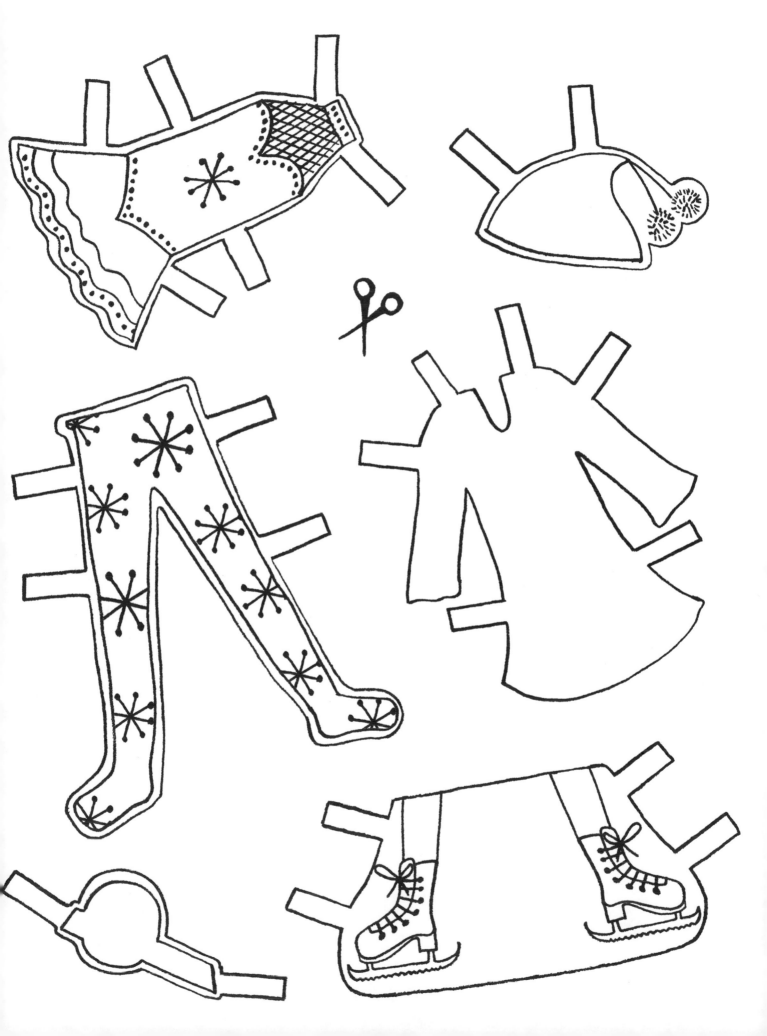

Perfect for pirouetting on the ice.

Get the dolls ready for a dancing competition.

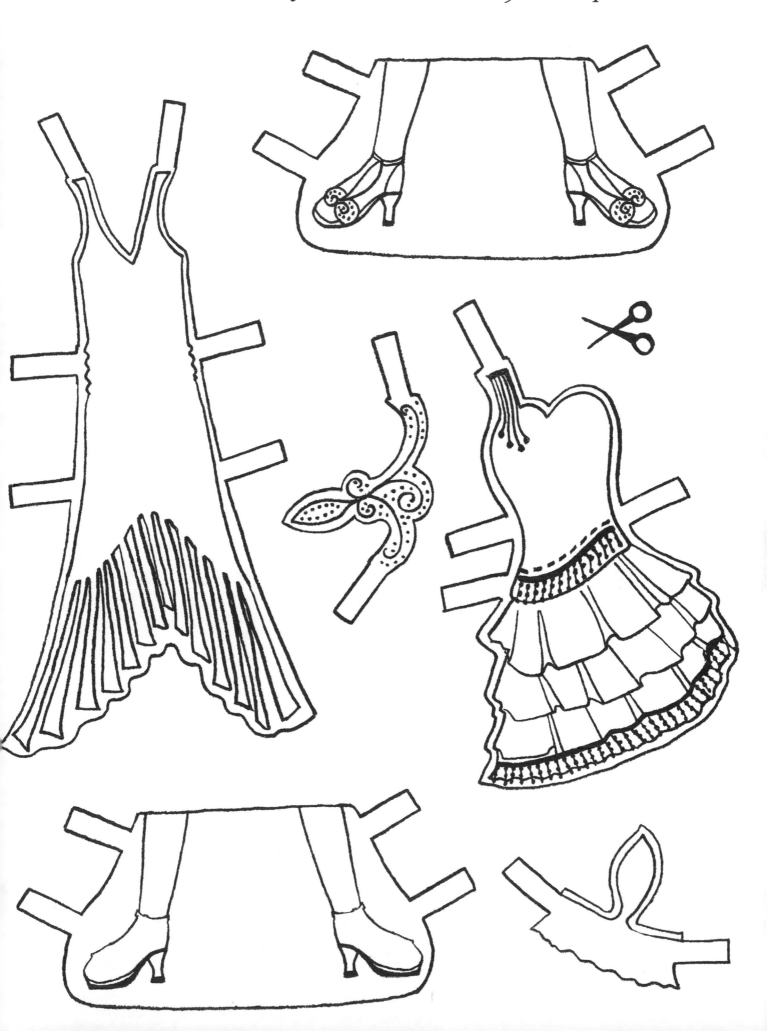

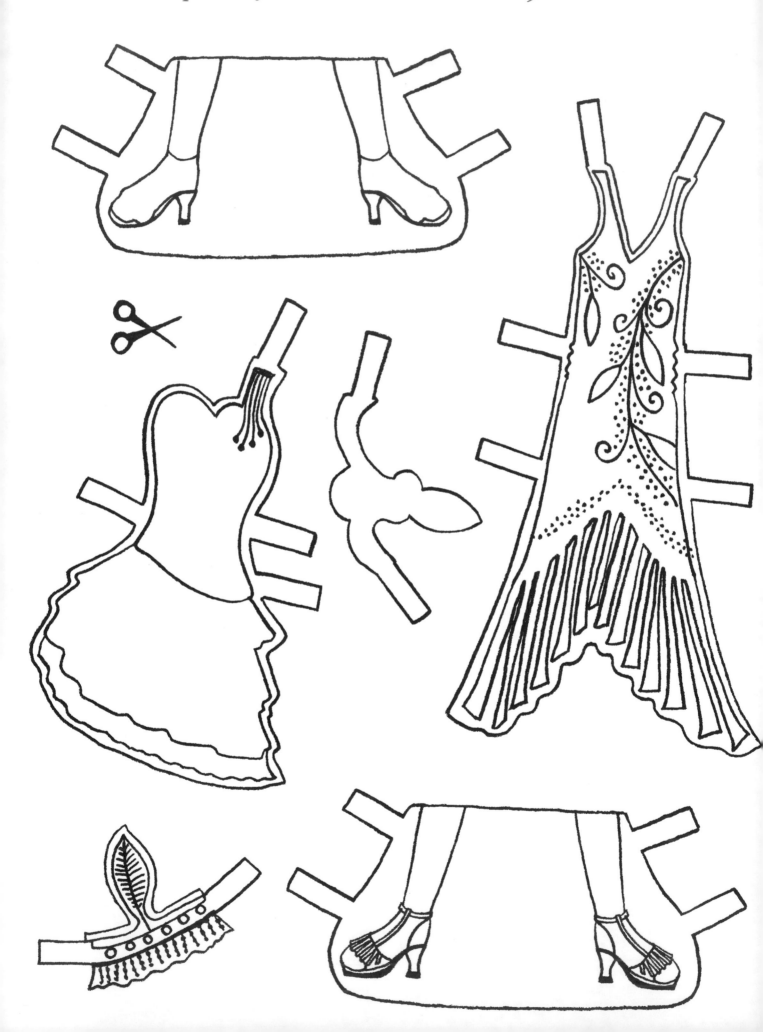

Cherry tries out for the cheerleading squad.

Doodle a winning cheerleading outfit.

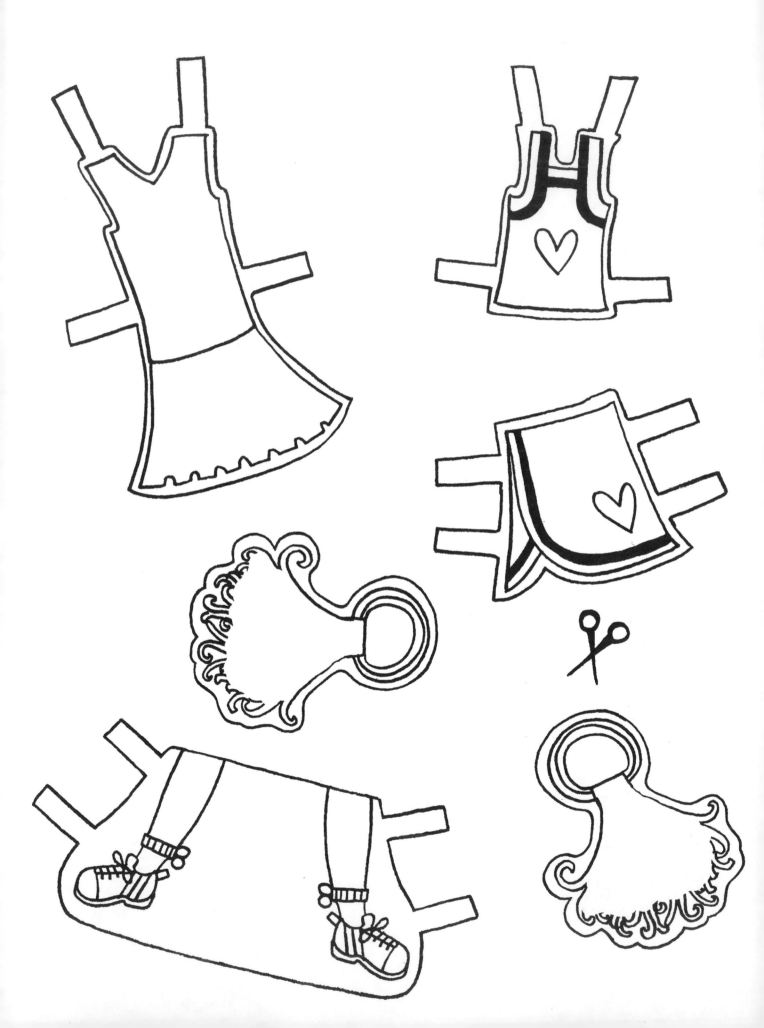

Who loves to do gymnastics?

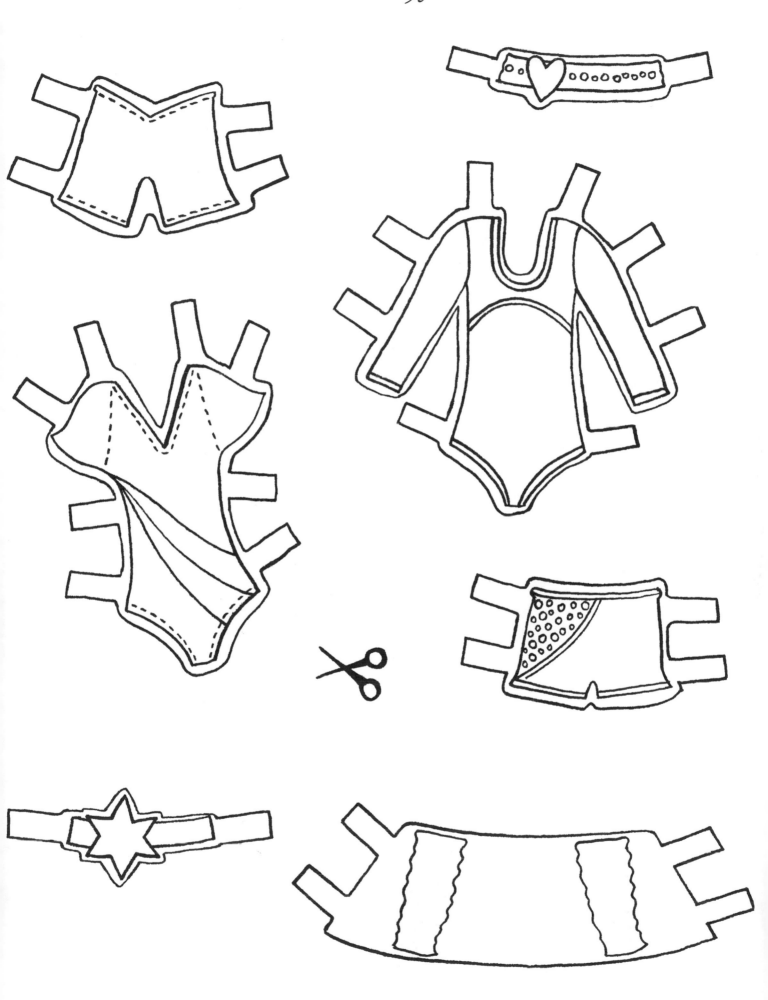

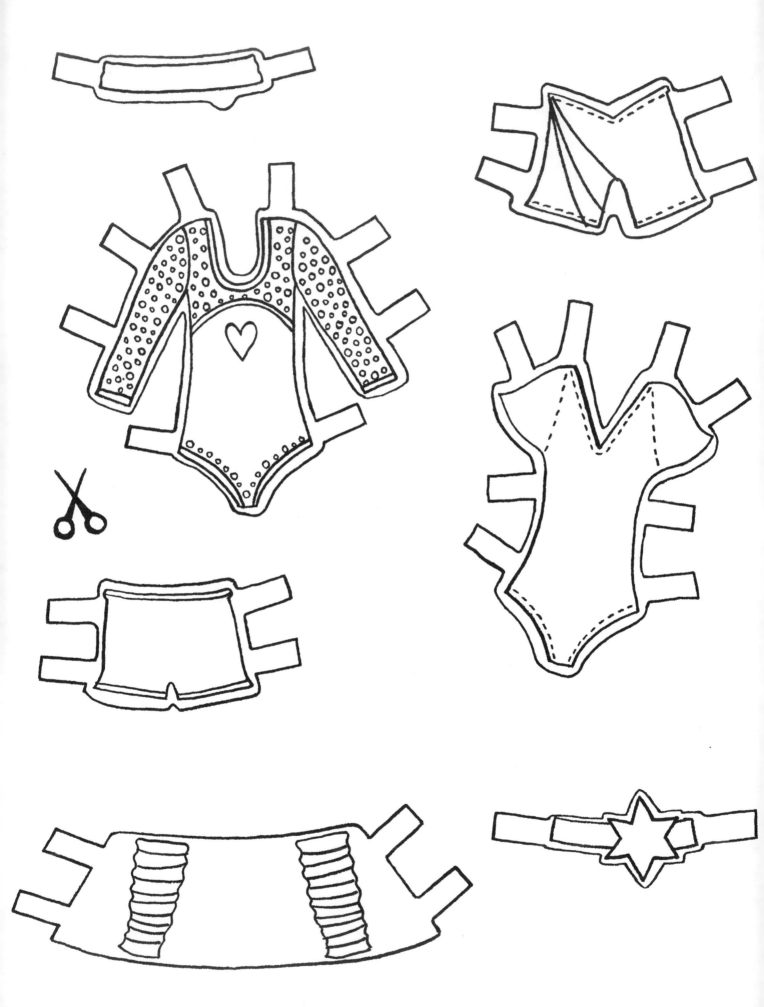

Dress one of the dolls for skiing.

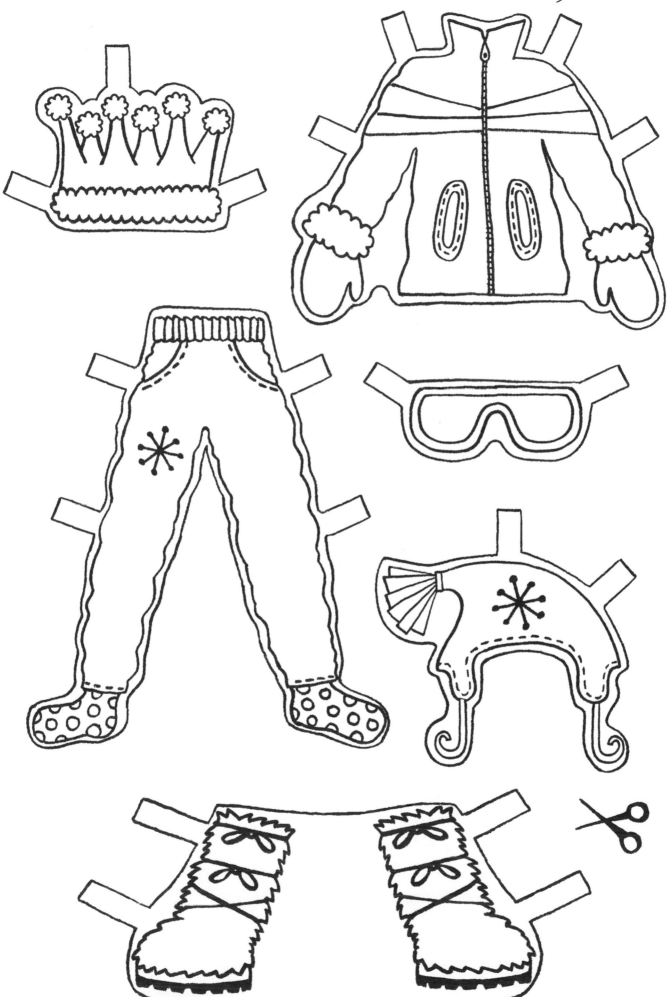

Sprinkle with snowflake patterns.

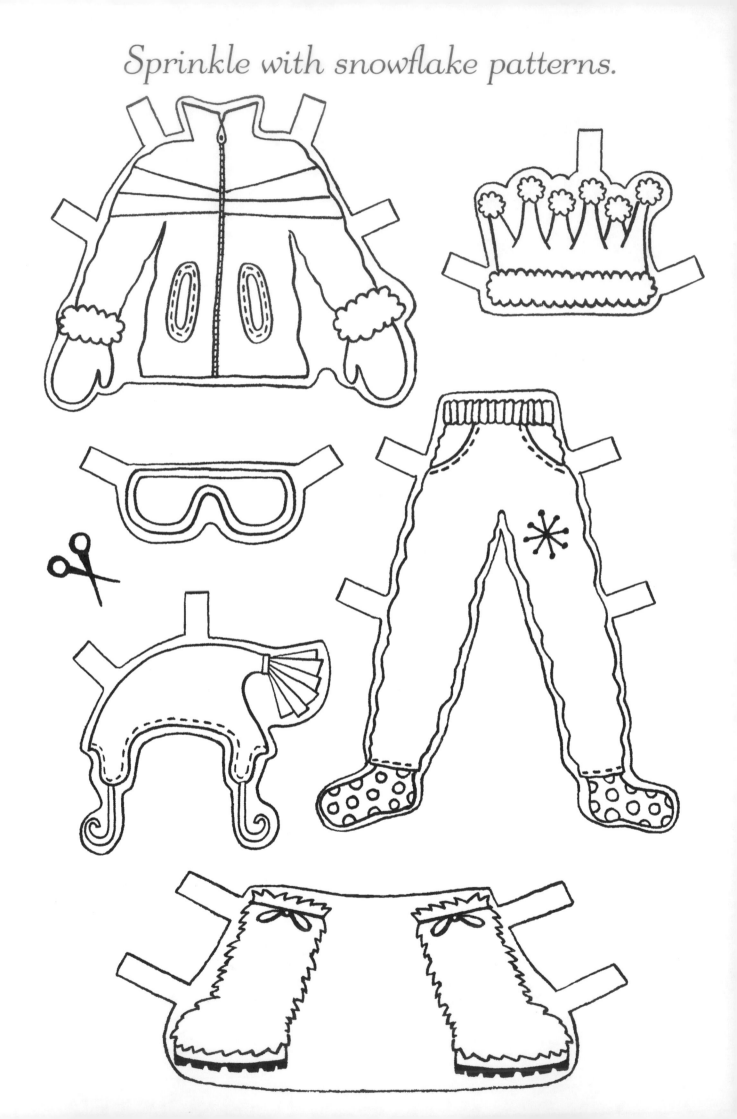

Miah wants to be a tennis champion.

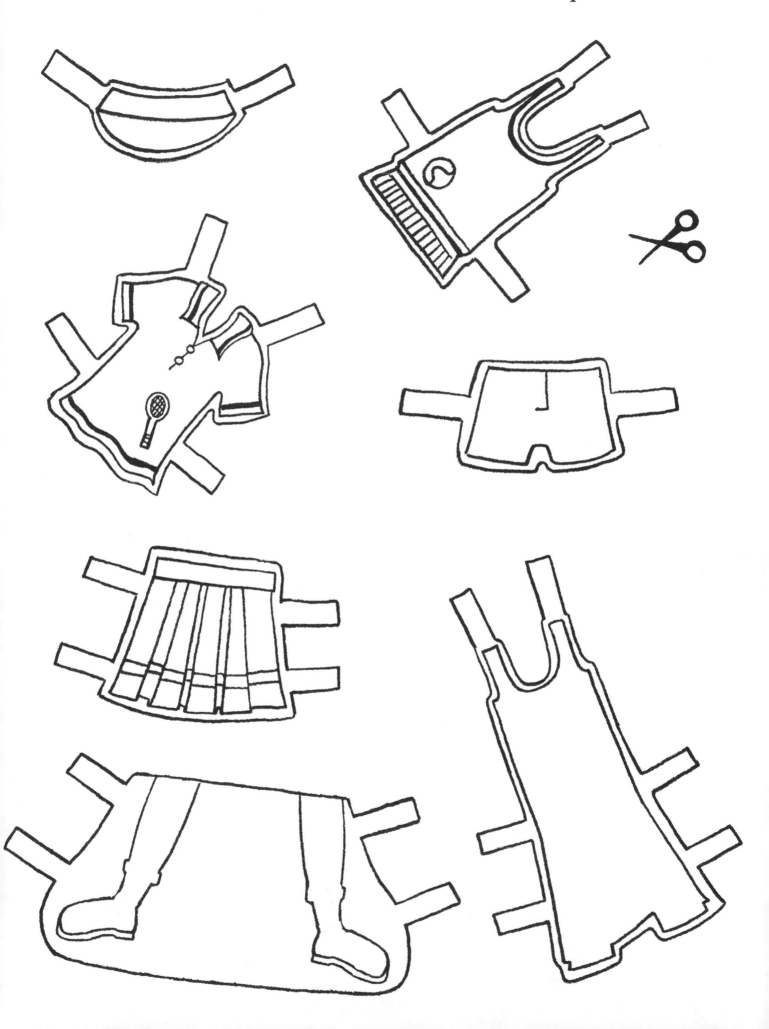

Ready to win matches.

THINGS TO GO WITH THE DOLLS' OUTFITS

Complete Miah's hat with lots of flowers.

The dolls need a hat for every occasion.

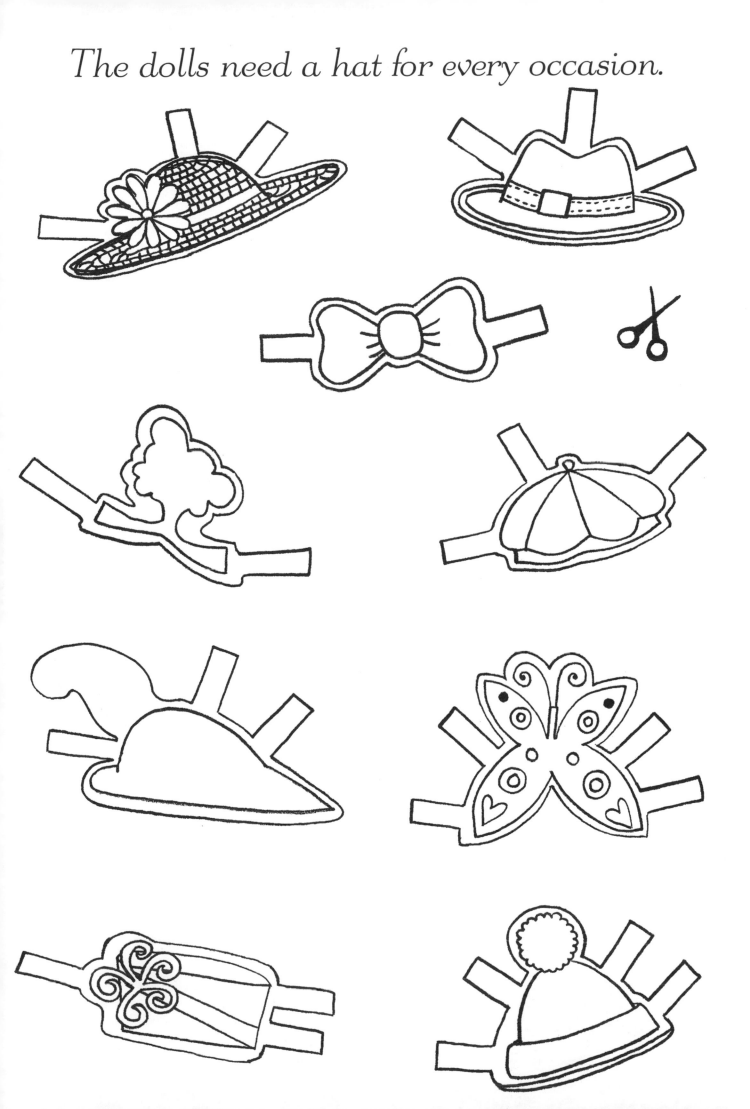

Hats off!

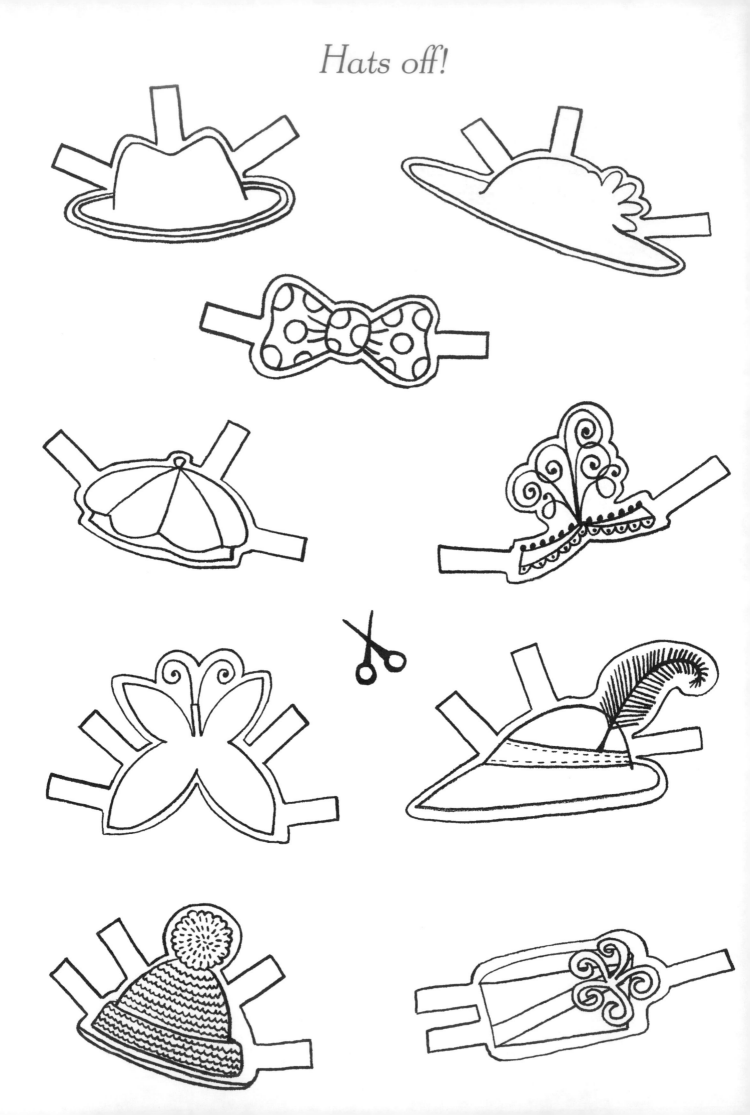

Decorate the dolls' favorite bags.

Give them bags of color.

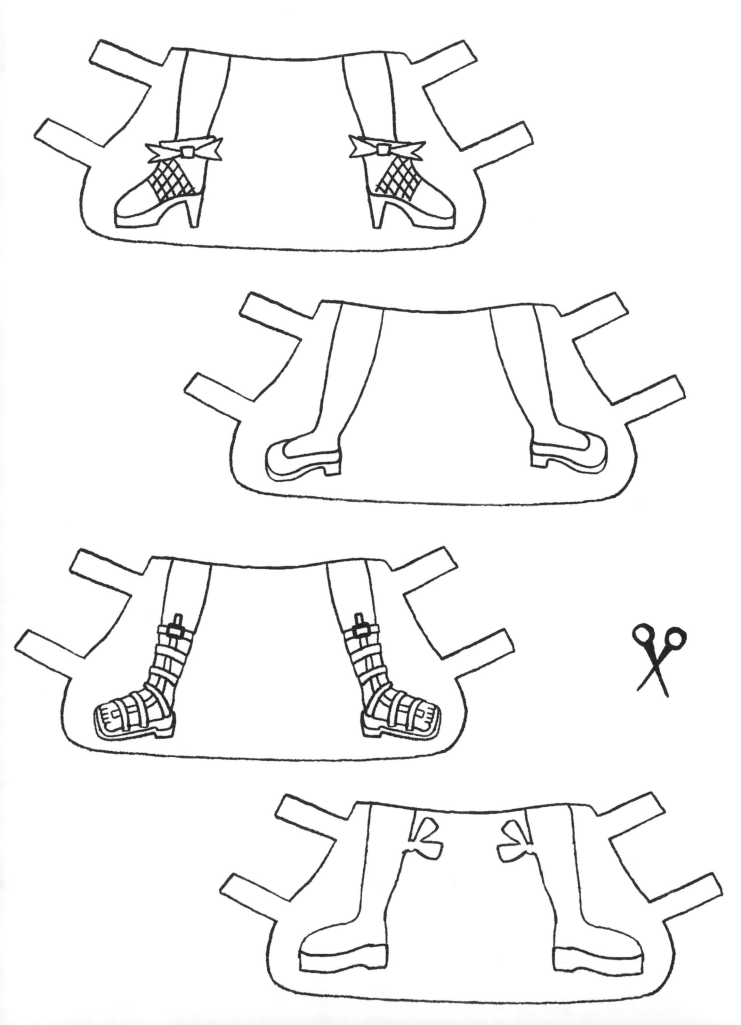

Make the shoes match the dolls' favorite outfits.

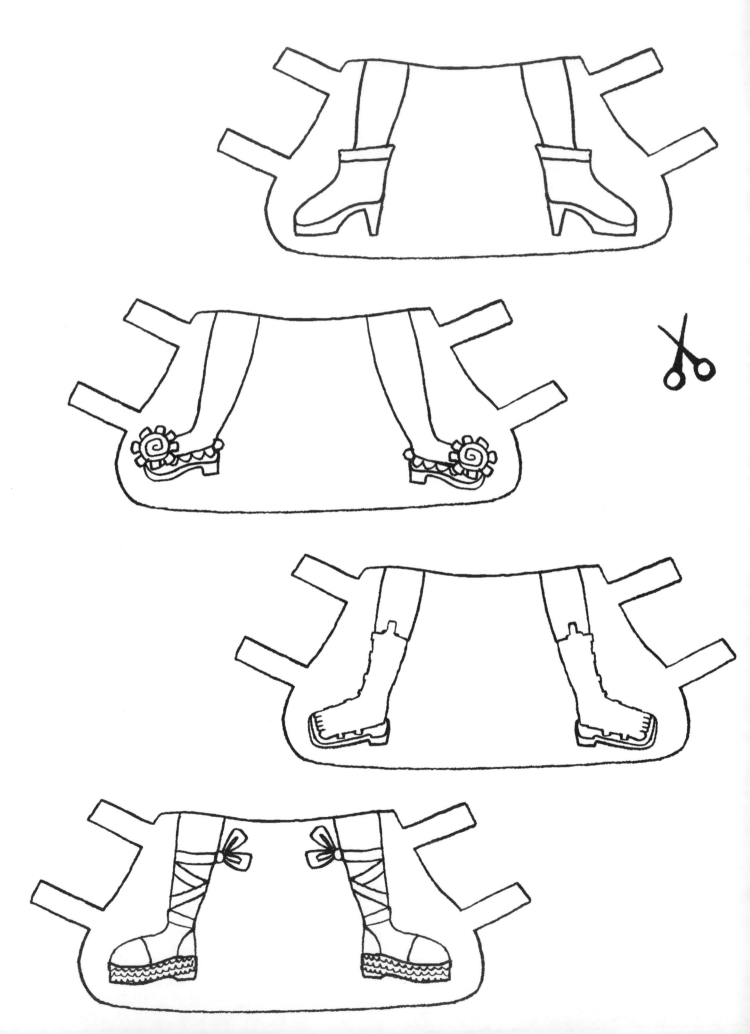

Complete the boots to keep the dolls' feet warm.

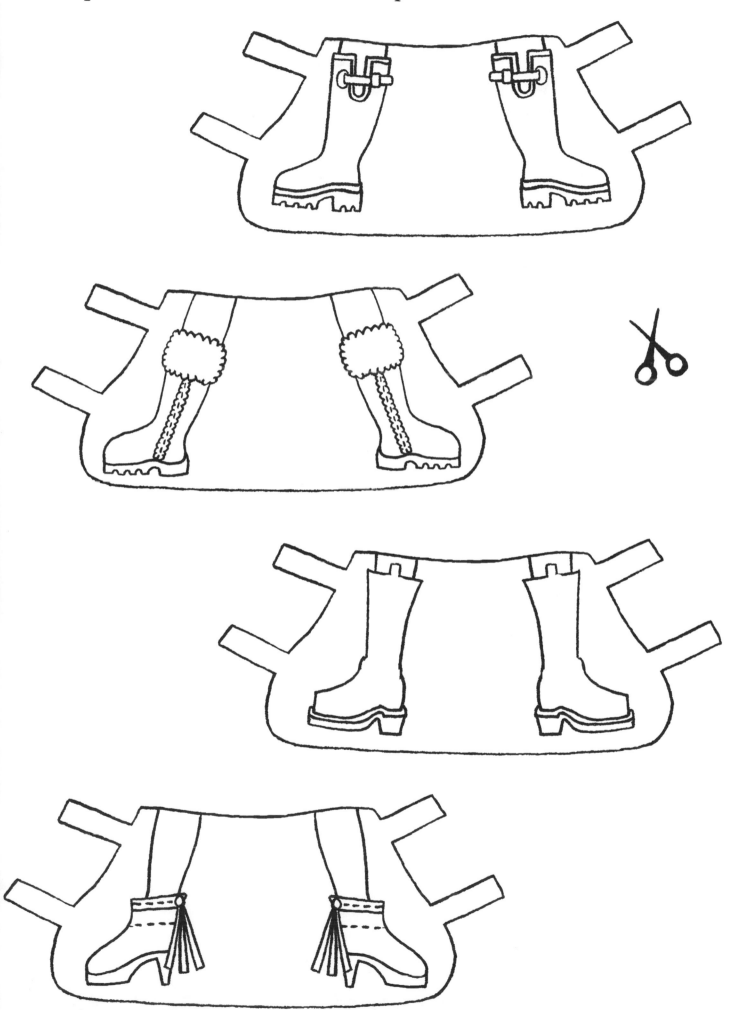

Add pretty patterns to match the outfits.

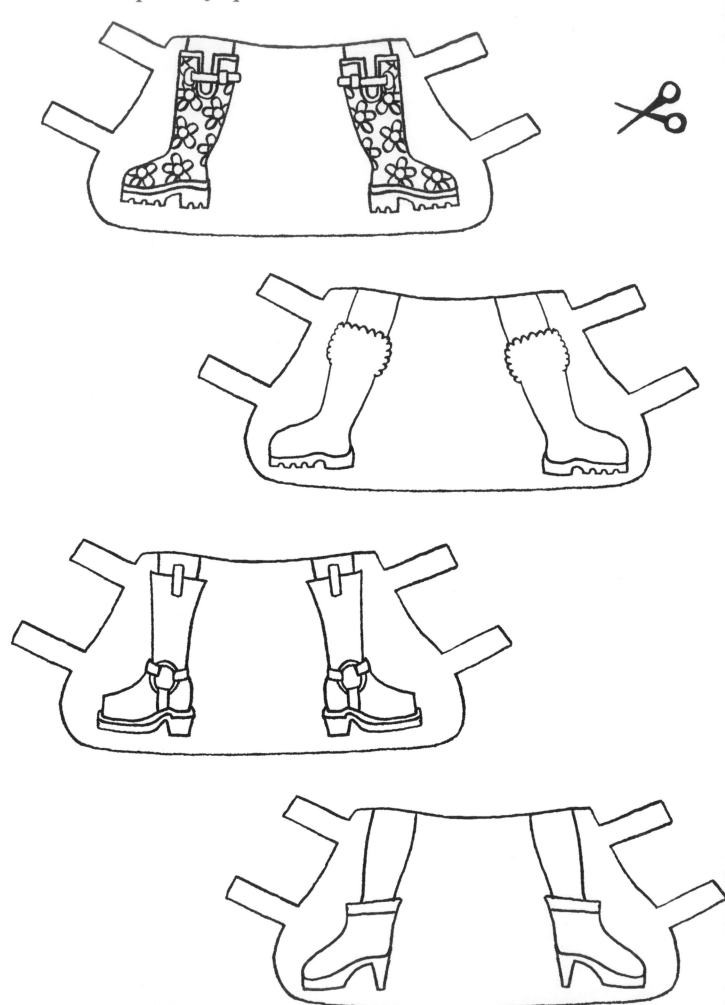

Super sunglasses.

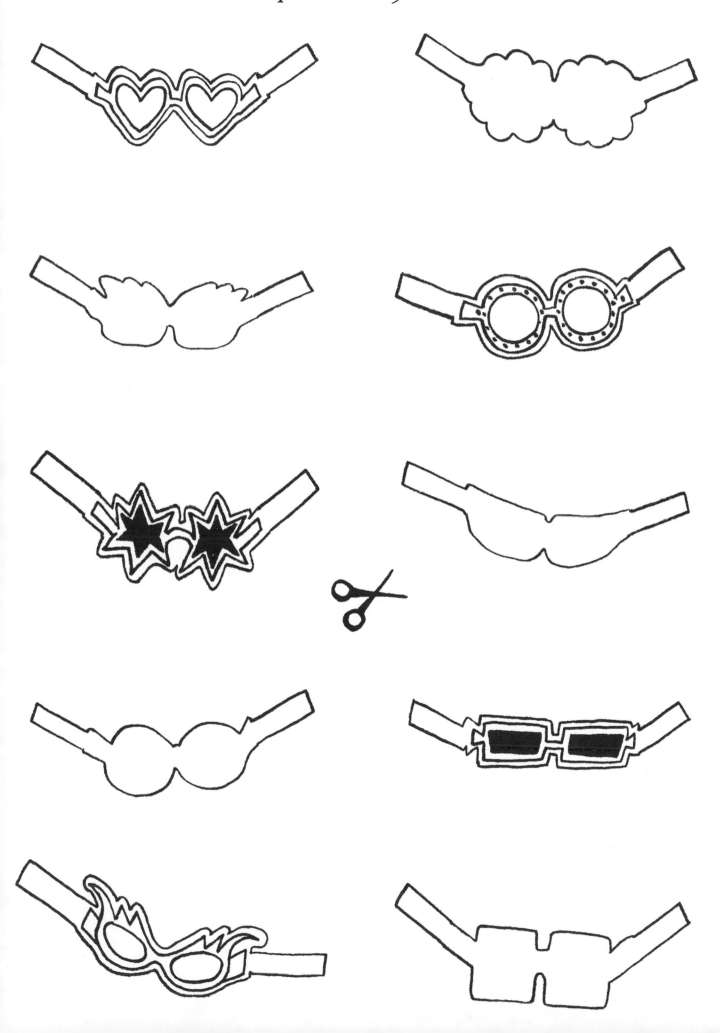

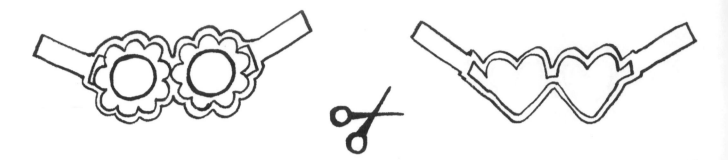

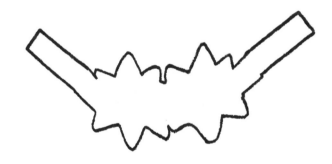

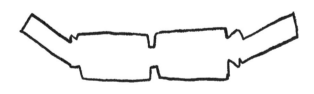

Design the cool T-shirts.

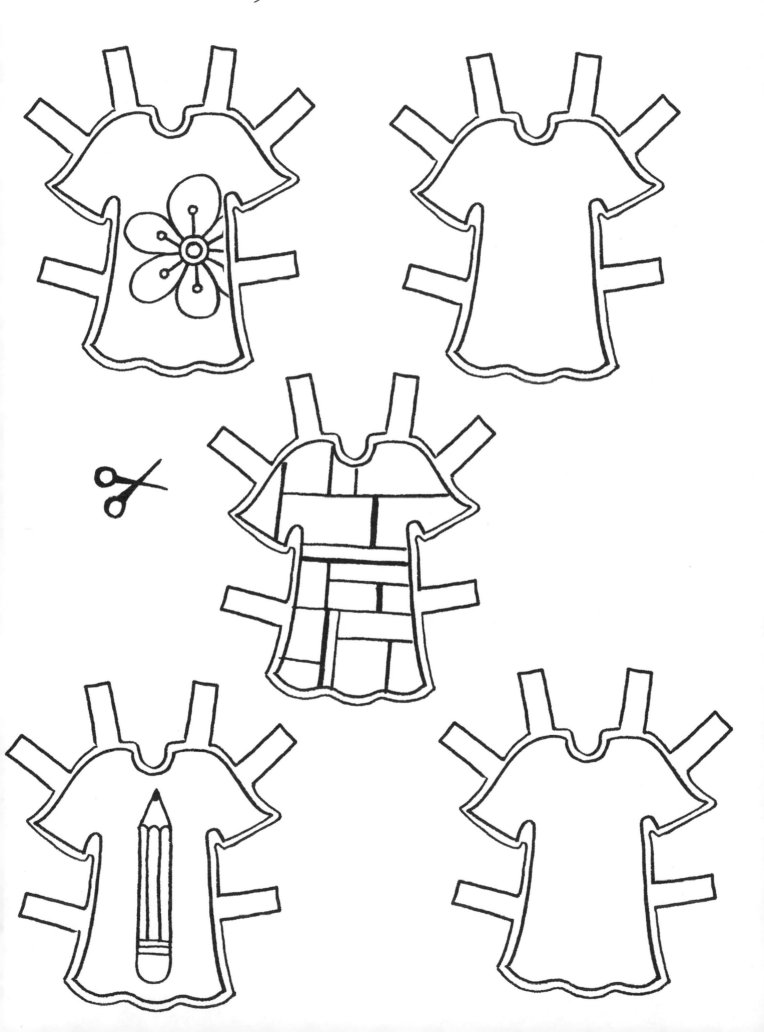

Complete with symbols and slogans.